The Berkshires Cookbook

The Berkshires Cookbook

Farm-Fresh Recipes from the Heart of Massachusetts

Jane Barton Griffith

Photography by Barbara Dowd

Globe
Pequot

Guilford, Connecticut

Globe Pequot

An imprint of Rowman & Littlefield

Distributed by NATIONAL BOOK NETWORK

Copyright © 2016 by Jane Barton Griffith
All photography copyright © 2016 by Barbara Dowd, unless otherwise noted

British Library Cataloguing in Publication Information Available

Library of Congress Cataloging-in-Publication Data

Griffith, Jane Barton, 1944- author.
  The Berkshires cookbook : farm-fresh recipes from the heart of Massachusetts / Jane Barton Griffith.
    pages cm
  Includes index.
  ISBN 978-1-4930-1260-2 (pbk. : alk. paper) — ISBN 978-1-4930-1655-6 (e-book) 1. Cooking, American—New England style. 2. Natural foods—Massachusetts—Berkshire Hills. 3. Local foods—Massachusetts—Berkshire Hills. 4. Seasonal cooking. I. Title.
  TX715.2.N48G76 2016
  641.5974—dc23

                                                                          2015036375

Contents

Introduction

The Berkshires and Pioneer Valley region are food hubs where the farmers and food producers are playing leading roles in the national sustainable food movement. The climate of excitement and innovation is reminiscent of the mood in California in the '70s when Alice Waters inspired a revolution in food. Food and farming are HOT and the Berkshires and Pioneer Valley are buzzing. Both seasoned and new farmers, many artisanal food producers and truly inspired chefs have collectively sparked a vibrant food scene.

When I was living in the Berkshires and working with Berkshire Mountain Bakery's master baker, Richard Bourdon, I found it stimulating to meet the farmers and artisan food makers, buying and cooking with their foods or tasting locally grown food in various restaurants. Inspired by all the fresh, delicious food, surrounded by passionate "locavore foodies" and creative chefs, I began writing this cookbook. The cookbook showcases eighty of my own recipes, organized by seasons, featuring the wonderful traditional and new foods found in the Berkshires and Pioneer Valley. I've added "special" ingredients or methods of preparation that will convert dishes from mundane to extraordinary, with subtle twists. All the recipes are simple to prepare—from taking a delicious

free-range egg and transforming it into a dinner delight with the help of Aleppo pepper or creating a vegetable dish with bulgur, mushrooms, and feta cheese, cooked in a parchment pouch. Some recipes belonged to my maternal or paternal family, others I borrowed or adapted from friends while most of them are original creations "cooked up" especially for this book.

To augment the eighty personal recipes, I am including contributions from Berkshire and Pioneer Valley farmers and food producers who kindly shared their recipes with me. Some of these people were already friends or colleagues while others I discovered through word-of-mouth referrals or research. When I interviewed, for example, the producers of Cricket Creek's artisanal cheeses or watched sap reducing into maple syrup at Mayval Farm, I asked them to if they would agree to contribute an "old-favorite" recipe. Another highlight in this cookbook is the inclusion of recipes from some of the best restaurants in the Berkshires and Pioneer Valley. The restaurants vary from a couple of high-end, exclusive restaurants with celebrity chefs to other more down-home, comfortable (and affordable) places with chefs who may not have attained national fame but who are cooking innovative food with exquisite flavors. My criteria for selecting restaurants and recipes for this book were not based on price of a meal, but the quality of the food and the chef's commitment to and passion for good local food.

Sometimes it took a lot of coaxing to obtain these closely held recipes. After e-mailing and calling a certain chef for six months, following an on-site interview and photo shoot, he still didn't send the recipes. I finally wrapped and shipped a precious jar of my rose hip jam with a note asking the chef if my jam might coax the recipes from him. The recipes came the next week.

Seasons

The recipes are organized by seasons, since each season is distinct in the Berkshires and Pioneer Valley. The seasons make us focus on what is locally grown and fresh. The seasons give definition and rhythm. Winter is quiet, therefore winter can call for quiet comfort food. When I need to think of a winter meal, I look at in the refrigerator to see what is available. Leeks and potatoes for a warm soup followed by a French apple tart? Perhaps. Or Brian Alberg of Red Lion might choose a big stew of meat and root vegetables since, Brian says, "winter is for pickling, canning, smoking, and stewing." I also like sitting around the fire with bowl of chestnut soup or a dish of polenta topped with meatballs in a tomato sauce based on the Coco and The Cellar Bar recipe in this book. In the winter, chefs and farmers in the Berkshires and Pioneer Valley are busy making sausages, putting bacon in the brine barrel, hanging meat in the smokehouse, curing meats with salt, herbs, spices, and sugar to cure or simmering them in a broth. Producing these delicacies brings a sense of creative fulfillment to the shortest days of the winter, and a bounty that will feed and sustain throughout the coldest weeks.

And when winter turns to spring, the whole region goes crazy for the first asparagus. Spring is often celebrated with over twenty-five regional restaurants participating in Farms + Foraging. The restaurants offer prix-fixe meals based on responsibly harvested, wild spring edibles from forests, fields, and farms. Taking a guided foraging walk called *Where the Wild Things Are* introduced me to ramps. Once I tasted ramps, I began to look for them at the local farmers' markets. One day when a Mennonite farmer was selling foraged ramps and morels, I balked at the price of the morels. Then I remembered the mantra in the Berkshires and Pioneer Valley, "Pay a bit more, eat better, and eat less." I bought them, went home, and cooked risotto with morels topped with grilled ramps. A simple, satisfying dish to highlight two extraordinary spring vegetables.

The summer is lush. The region is green with its trees and fields. If the fields aren't green with plants and grains, there are often whole fields that are mowed into green velvet spaces. The summer brings an abundance of exceptional produce. The tomatoes want to be eaten in the field,

or immediately upon being purchased, with the sweet juice running down the arm that holds the tomato. As many as thirty varieties of microgreens are offered at local farmers' markets. Microgreens are tender baby plants that are highly nutritious because, as sprouts, they contain all the nutrients that will be dispersed throughout a mature plant. One type of microgreen that ignited me was corn sprouts. They were as flavorful as an ear of corn. There were also special summer treats at the local farmers' markets. I bought my first "baby ginger" and befriended a mushroom grower and oohed and aahed over her yellow oyster mushrooms.

It is always a bit sad to see the summer, with fresh lettuce and corn, disappear. Yet the fall season with its colored foliage and abundant produce is also spectacular in this region. A particular show of red and gold leaves against the shockingly blue "Indian Summer" sky could cause me to catch my breath. The fall brings a wealth of new vegetables—my favorite Russian kale, which flourishes in cooler temperatures, plus all the root vegetables I delight in learning to appreciate and cook. I combine kohlrabi, turnips, and parsnips into delicious dishes or bake old-favorite squashes like acorn and kabocha with a wee bit of sage and maple syrup. Beans are soaked and turned into cassoulets. When the ground is covered with acorns, I think about the benefits of nuts, which inspired me to include my friend Gabriel's recipe for harvest crackers in the book. These crackers are perfect fall appetizers when served with cheese or a great protein snack for a fall hike.

Many countries celebrate the arrival and life span of certain seasonal foods. All over Europe regions highlight their foods with feasts, parades, and restaurant specials. In the US, where most foods are available flown in and sort-of-fresh or frozen year-round, we haven't developed the same appreciation for—or celebration of—local seasonal foods.

The Berkshire and Pioneer Valley chefs and farmers are changing this by highlighting seasonal foods and educating us about these foods. Clarkdale Farms participates in one of the big apple festivals in the Pioneer Valley. Residents in the region and visitors from nearby areas used to come to these festivals for their kids to have fun on the moon-bounce or purchase freshly pressed cider. A major change has occurred. Farmers are offering all sorts of heritage breed apples with

distinctive tastes and crunch. And now customers are coming to find these wonderful apples and to ask questions. The dialogue between farmers and consumers is intense. The apple festivals have morphed into an educational and buying opportunity as well as a time to be outside in the fall. I have included a recipe for "cheese" made from quince apples. Look for that fall window of time when quince apples are sold and follow the recipe to make a special, translucent, rosy-orange quince paste. Quince paste is enjoyed in Europe and South America and now it is finally being appreciated in the Berkshires and Pioneer Valley. As one farmer commented to me when I asked for quince apples, "Two years ago I couldn't give away those ugly things."

To celebrate the seasons, besides my recipes and the recipes from farmers, artisanal food producers, and chefs, I include a food tour at the end of each seasonal chapter. I list farms that encourage visits, a baker who bakes heritage, whole-grain breads in a wood-burning oven, a shop that sells homemade world-class chocolates, a butcher who makes his own charcuterie and, of course, restaurants and cafes that offer phenomenal dishes made with locally grown food. Food artisans are making breads, roasting coffees, growing wines, and setting up tables end to end to create "pop-up" restaurants in the midst of fields. You can find them listed in the seasonal tours information.

The Berkshire and Pioneer Valley areas are known for their cultural heritage—from the Clark Art Institute, MASS MoCA, and the Williamstown Theatre Festival to Deerfield, with its historic houses and fine museums. The Berkshires has long attracted New Yorkers and Bostonians, who have bought summer residences. Now it is common to see tourists from Europe and eastern Canada. The major change that has occurred in the last five years is that now the Berkshires and Pioneer Valley are a food destination and a top attraction for visitors interested in savoring and absorbing the "vibe" of the food scene.

Good, Clean Fair Food

As I worked on this book, buying local ingredients from the farmers or farm stands and creating recipes, people often asked me how to define the Berkshire and Pioneer Valley food movement, questioned me about who was involved and why the movement was happening in this region. This local, regional scene in western and mid-state Massachusetts is a manifestation of—and a connection to—a global effort called the International Slow Food Movement. The motto of the Slow Food Movement perfectly describes the goal of Berkshire and Pioneer Valley farmers and food makers: "Good, Clean, Fair." Good means fresh and flavorful. Clean stands for no herbicides, pesticides, or genetically modified organisms (GMO). Fair stands for fair market value—including decent pay for farmworkers and recognition that organic or artisanal food may cost more.

Started in the 1980s by Carlo Petrini in Italy, the Slow Food movement mission is to maintain traditional foods as part of Italian culture and family life. Plus, the small farms that dot the countryside are visually beautiful and preserve a historic landscape that is vital to the tourist economy. Fast life was leading to fast food and a dwindling interest in food, knowledge of where it comes from, or how food choices were affecting the environment. The catalyst for Petrini occurred when McDonald's planned to open a fast-food restaurant across from the Spanish Steps in Rome. Petrini considers it vital that Italians embrace and maintain their traditions of eating local sustainably raised foods for taste and "gastronomic pleasure" and at meals that gather friends and family to eat together. If the celebration of food disappeared, it would cause the degeneration of intimacy among friends and family and a loss of respect for the older generation. Also, part of the Slow Food Movement's mission is to save heritage plants, trees, and foods that are endangered, because special foods of a region evoke flavor-food memories and are important to biodiversity. The Slow Food movement caught on in Italy, where "slow food" is a common and recognized term. There are trattorias specializing in local slow food and a growing popularity for agritourism, which promotes farm-stays with dining based solely on farm-raised or local food. The International Slow Food movement is active in 160 countries with millions of members.

The Slow Food movement's "good, clean, fair" mission and building communities that care about food are unifying themes for the farmers, food producers, and chefs in the Berkshires and Pioneer Valley. For example, one Berkshire farm website, Moon in the Pond, states, "At the center—food is about the feeding and caring of others—your family and community and building strong, respectful enduring relationships with both the people and the land." Yes, farmers and food producers want to make money and become successful, but they demonstrate a deep commitment to sharing and supporting one another. Berkshire Farm & Table, an association created to promote a collection of local farms, artisan food makers, and chefs, produced a video documentary (which includes some of the chefs and artisan food producers mentioned in this book) and each person ends his or her interview with, "It's my backyard." That speaks of how they feel about food and community. As one Pioneer Valley chef explained to me, "We seem to avoid conflict because everyone agrees that teamwork brings benefit. We know that what is good for one, is good for all."

Leadership

The people who are making the food revolution happen in the Berkshires and Pioneer Valley are established farmers with forty years of commitment to the land, and an extraordinary blend of idealistic, committed young people with a passion for food. I tell some of the stories of both the senior and younger people who are having a great impact on the food scene in this book. Here I will talk about three farmers providing leadership—Elizabeth Keen of Indian Line Farm, Dominic Palumbo of Moon in the Pond Farm, and Dan Barber of Blue Hill Farm and Restaurant. Each is bringing an entrepreneurial approach to farming and food, and each is involved with mentoring young farmers and artisanal food producers.

Elizabeth Keen: In its desire to save one of the first Community Supported Agriculture (CSA) programs in the country, the Berkshires community, the Nature Conservancy, and a local land trust used an example of the type of entrepreneurial approach I discuss in the book. These three entities partnered to place the Indian Line Farm in a trust to maintain it as a working farm after its original owner died. When the Indian Line Farm experimented with a CSA in the 1980s, no one had heard of this concept. A CSA offered shares, or membership, in the farm in exchange for an offering of farm produce. The upfront money permits the farms to buy seed or equipment, and the guaranteed income from the CSAs makes it easier for the farm's business planning. When the CSAs first began at Indian Line Farm, the boxes might occasionally contain too many of some odd vegetable, but now the customers usually have a long list of tempting vegetables, herbs, fruits, and flowers to select from. Today, utilizing smart marketing strategies, Indian Line Farm offers several options for CSA shares to 140 families: year-round or summer-only CSA shares. These shares can be just for vegetables, with additional offerings of fruits and/or flowers. There is even a "working share," which allows a customer to work on the farm to offset the cost of a portion of the share.

Another innovative solution at Indian Line Farm caught my attention. Many small farms, like Indian Line Farm, face the problem of not being able to afford the cost and legal requirements of becoming a USDA certified organic farm. Some of these smaller and medium-size farms encouraged the founding of a nonprofit that provides label certification and oversight to farms that follow organic practices. The label "Certified Naturally Grown" guarantees that all products adhere to all USDA organic methods and requirements. And of course, Indian Line Farm mentors apprentices and welcomes regular volunteers.

Dan Barber: Dan grew up in the Berkshires, and he still owns, with his brother, the family farm called Blue Hill Farm (see Spring Season profile). Thanks to the farm manager, Sean Stanton, the farm provides meat, vegetables, and savory yogurt to the award-winning Blue Hill Restaurant in New York City and the equally good restaurant, Blue Hill at Stone Barns Center for Food and Agriculture, a nonprofit center and educational facility in Westchester County, New York, which promotes sustainable agriculture. Dan was selected by *Time* magazine as one of the most influential thinkers in the US for the year 2009, and it is easy to understand why, if you read any of his books or listen to his TED talks.

Dan's recent manifesto, *The Third Plate*, challenges the premise that eating "local will reshape the landscape and drive lasting change." Dan explains that "Big Food is getting Bigger with 1.1 percent of farms generating 45 percent of farm revenue." Fortunately for the environment and food lovers, Dan is vigorously exploring and researching ways to find solutions for our nation's agricultural crisis. Dan offers multiple examples of sustainable agriculture approaches. In one example, Dan cites a farmer who keeps his land rich without fertilizers by using cover crops like mustard greens, barley, and kidney beans. Using these "place-holding crops" to restore the land for cash crops will be a problem until, Dan suggests, serious, well-paying markets can be created for cover crops.

Dan takes complex agricultural issues, explains them in thoughtful, layperson's language. Dan's rare perspective and exceptional cuisine is inspirational. Dan challenges the existing state of food in America yet offers encouragement for the survival of the environment based on entrepreneurial strategies and experience he has gathered from various individuals around the world. Dan's great reverence for how plants are grown and animals raised and his interpretation of cuisine based on seasonal, local, and organic food have elevated Dan to a position of leadership in the food movement. The annual Young Farmers Conference at Stone Barns draws hundreds of new farmers who want to learn from Dan and others like him.

Dominic Palumbo: Dominic is the owner of Moon in the Pond Farm, which utilizes an interesting model for farm operation. He has established the farm as a nonprofit entity with 99 percent of the farm revenue supporting its educational mission and 1 percent contributed to 1% for the Planet, an alliance of 1,100 members in 48 countries who commit 1 percent of their sales to environmental causes.

There are now two currencies in the Berkshires. One, called Berkshares, saves a customer 5 percent on purchases in the Berkshires at the many places that accept the currency, from the Red Lion Inn to retail stores or farmers' markets. Although it accepts Berkshares, Moon in the Pond has created its own currency called Bacon Bucks. Bacon Bucks aren't just for meat. They can be used for any of the products sold by Moon in the Pond at any of their locations—from Moon in the Pond Farm to any of the farmers' markets or outlets that carry their produce. And the Bacon Shares have no expiration date. They are truly "a deal."

The goal of the farm is to grow organic heirloom vegetables and fruits, humanely raise grass-fed heritage animals, and educate aspiring farmers and students. A Kickstarter effort raised funds for a stipend for a Young Farmer, who was selected from a pool of highly competitive applicants. The Young Farmer will spend one year learning and working on the farm. Moon in the Pond Farm offers apprenticeships for full-year or seasonal terms and, in addition, the farm accepts a certain number of farmworkers, known as "Woofers," with the World-Wide Opportunities on Organic Farms (WWOOF). All of those who come to work at Moon in the Pond are educated to comprehend and deal with the complexities of a diverse, sustainable farm system like that at Moon in the Pond. The farm offers multiple tours for public and private schools: Open Gate, a self-guided tour for visitors; and a two-hour fee-based educational tour and guided tour and talk by Dominic Palumbo. In addition to their CSA program, Moon in the Pond sells produce at several farmers' markets and Rubiner's Store, an outstanding cheesemonger in Great Barrington, Massachusetts. Farmer Dom, as he is affectionately called, is a visionary whose curiosity, drive, and perseverance have built the strong farming experience that he is now passing on to the younger generation.

Apprentices and New Farmers

The Pioneer Valley has one of the highest concentrations of higher educational institutions in the country, and many of these schools have courses that provide students with the theoretical and practical tools they need to understand food production and its relationship to the environment. After all, this is a generation of young people who are concerned with the environment, and many students become involved with the politics of food, which often leads to activism and direct involvement with food production, including farming. As one farmer told me, "Farming is a political act. Eating is an agricultural act. Young people are disgusted with the corporate dominance over food production and seeking new solutions for how food is raised, delivered, and eaten. Being involved with food and community is their way of building their own wholesome world. These young people who have chosen to farm fully appreciate that farming is tough work—day in and day out hard work. At the same time, they feel fulfilled by the honest, dirty toil of farming, as well as seeing their mission as greater than farming alone."

Many small and mid-size farms have been saved, thanks to the young people, college educated or not, who come to work on the farms. Many of them fall within the apprenticeship system. The candidates are selectively chosen for positions on farms and then they agree to work and learn for a period of time, usually for a minimal stipend, free food, and housing. The most successful apprenticeships programs are those in which the aspiring farmers are provided with serious training and a transfer of skills by the mentoring farmer in exchange for the apprentices' inexpensive labor. One tongue-in-cheek job description for apprentices states, "Apprentices can expect to muck, mulch, milk, mow, herd, hay, harvest, hoe, water, weed, weed, seed, feed, fence, fix, forage, clean, weed, plant, transplant, tidy, weed, clean, scrub, pick, stake, rake, wash, weed, build, record, sweep, swear, study, organize, observe, report, clean, cry, compost, cook, swear, laugh, laugh, and laugh." Most farms have full-time slots for a few apprentices, and they accept additional shorter-term apprentices for the growing and farmers' market seasons.

Most farms encourage apprentices to participate in the regional **Collaborative Regional Alliance for Farmer Training (CRAFT)** programs. The apprentices will gather at a select farm, where the farmer will share the expertise of his or her particular farm or artisanal food-making process. This enables apprentices to broaden their experience and skill set beyond their personal farm experience and provides a peer base for connecting with others who share similar goals. And meeting their peers has led to the scheduling of "weed dating" (a play on the term speed dating) events for apprentices to meet each other. The popularity of apprenticeship programs has had a strong impact on farms across the country but particularly in the Berkshires and Pioneer Valley. Here, due to the farms' close proximity to one another, the apprentices are able to form a sense of community and common purpose.

Importance of Technology

The most profound impact on the agricultural and food production in the Berkshires and Pioneer Valley can be credited to technology and entrepreneurial approaches. Together, these rescued the "family farm." Though the region was home to generations of farming families and especially fertile soil, the farms were dying fast. Then, with the arrival of the Internet, the situation changed. The Internet presented the farmer with a sophisticated marketing tool and access to wider markets, which have increased sales. Today nearly every farm has its own website where customers can learn more about the farm's history, review produce offerings with a seasonal schedule, see photos of the farms, usually with lots of photos of irresistible baby animals. Blogs allow customers to communicate and stay informed about the goings-on at the farm. The two most important marketing outcomes, facilitated by the Internet, were the creation of farmers' markets and CSAs. Both

give the farmers direct access to their customers. For example, CSA customers can look up the schedule (and weather-impacted variations) of when certain foods will be available, order weekly allotments, and even find recipes for the vegetables or fruits arriving in their CSA box. The interaction between farmer and customer is mutually beneficial. Customers learn more about their food and their farmers, and gain an appreciation of a higher quality and flavor in food, while the farmers can educate their customers and become more responsive to their needs.

The Internet directly benefits the farmer as an educational tool. One baker talked about "the old days" when he would try to reach a colleague by phone to locate certain heritage grains or ask questions when he was having difficulties with his sourdough starter. Now the answers are on the Internet, and communications are nearly instantaneous. Sean Stanton, of Blue Hill Farm and Restaurant, told me that he gained a lot of his farming experience researching, reading, and watching videos on the Internet. The Internet permits farmers to locate educational workshops or grant opportunities. Farmers and food producers have created their own organizations, such as Berkshire Grown, to promote themselves and their activities mostly via the Internet. Although there is still room for growth and improvement, the Internet is connecting farmers directly with restaurants and other facilities that serve food, like schools or hospitals, for farm-to-fork buying. In several cases, farms were saved from development thanks to online "activism." The ability to go beyond the fence of the farm via the Internet has brought these small family farms to the world. Fortunately, with the heightened interest in wholesome, healthy, tasty food, the farmers are being met with a highly receptive audience.

Region

The term "the Berkshires" is understood, by most people, to refer to the hilly-mountainous region of western Massachusetts. The elevation was formed over half a billion years ago when the continent of Africa collided with North America, pushing up the Appalachian Mountains, part of which run through the Berkshires, and forming the bedrock of the Berkshires. The Pioneer Valley is the name given to the portion of the Connecticut River Valley that is located in Massachusetts. The heart of the Pioneer Valley is the Connecticut River—which cuts the valley—and the adjacent "hills" on both sides.

It is interesting to examine why this food revolution is happening in the Berkshires and Pioneer Valley. One reason is its fertile soil. When glaciers receded, water was trapped over much of this area and, as the water evaporated, sediments were deposited in the soil. Think of it as cooking down a sauce to its "essence" when the richest part of the liquid remains. Minerals and organic matter were deposited in the soil, coloring much of the soil in the region a dark black. The Berkshires and Pioneer Valley have the richest soil in all of New England, which is one reason why this region boasts that it is the highest food-producing area in the New England states. The rich soil attracted European settlers as early as 1635. Farms that have been in the same families for multiple generations flourished until the era of "corporate agriculture." Fortunately, families like the Mayval Farm, founded by the Parsons family in 1778, held tight, determined to survive, until the arrival of the Slow Food Movement and technological advances opened new avenues and affected attitudes toward locally grown food that helped Mayval Farm survive.

Building on its history of family farms and the quality of soil due to the glaciers, "old is now new." Centennial farms still utilizing traditional farming practices, while adding innovative methods, sophisticated marketing practices and entrepreneur approaches, are now bringing their food to wider markets and customers to the farm. This cookbook attempts to describe the regional food movement in the Berkshires and Pioneer Valley and explain why it is generating a vibrant community for locals, second-home owners—and visitors.

Fall

Small Plate

Cranberry Mostarda

4–6 SERVINGS

Tart in taste and stunning in color, cranberries are one of the indigenous fruits of North America. Native Americans utilized cranberries as food, healing medicine for wounds and preventive medicine due to its high vitamin C content and antioxidant level. It was a terrible fate that caused this magnificent berry to end up as a firm gunk of cranberry jelly that slides out of an opened can . . . shhwooosh, shlug, splat into a serving bowl. Don't buy that canned jelly. Try this traditional Italian condiment that mixes fruits and mustard. The Italians serve it with charcuterie or cheese, or with grilled chicken, steak, pork, lamb, and sausages.

Though most people think of Cape Cod as the source of all cranberries, they are grown commercially in lots of places in the Pioneer Valley and Berkshires.

½ cup sugar

⅜ cup light brown sugar

⅛ cup dry mustard

1 tablespoon Dijon mustard

¾ cup orange juice or small orange pulverized in
    food processor

⅛ cup lemon juice

1 small onion, minced

½ cup dry white wine

3 tablespoons white wine vinegar

3 tablespoons water

1 tablespoon unsalted butter

12 ounces cranberries

Spices:

1 teaspoon allspice

1 teaspoon ground ginger

⅛ teaspoon cayenne pepper

2 whole cloves

Small cinnamon stick

1 star anise

4 juniper berries or 2 bay leaves

To make the mostarda: Combine white and brown sugar, two mustards, orange and lemon juice, onion, white wine, wine vinegar, water, butter, and all the spices in a saucepan. Bring to a boil and then reduce to a simmer for 30 minutes. Add the cranberries and continue to cook over low heat, stirring occasionally, until the cranberries have popped. Simmer until the mostarda is jam-like, 2 to 3 minutes longer. Serve the mostarda warm or chilled.

The mostarda will keep for a month or two in the refrigerator. Placed in a jar with a ribbon, this condiment is a nice gift.

Brunch

Egg White Wrap
with Oyster Mushrooms and Spinach

SERVES 4

One of my best friends, Glenda, is a wise, kind woman who possesses many healthy recipes and natural cures passed down to her from her grandmother who lived to 114 and raised fourteen girls! You better believe this recipe is nutritious for you! Plus, Glenda and I have been researching the benefits of mushrooms, one of the most undervalued food items in America. Americans have been slow to appreciate mushrooms because of our limited exposure to any type of interesting varieties. All over the Berkshires and Pioneer Valley, experts are foraging mushrooms, sharing their knowledge, and selling mushrooms at the farmers' markets. While raising oyster mushrooms, I have become enchanted with their delicate oyster taste. My mushrooms come in bright yellow, gray, and white. If you can find yellow oyster mushrooms, they make a great presentation in this simple dish.

6 egg whites
1 tablespoon butter
3 tablespoons olive oil
1 tablespoon minced onion
½ pound oyster mushrooms or cremini, sliced
1 pound spinach, stems removed and torn into pieces
¼ cup sour cream
2 tomatoes, minced very fine

To prepare the white omelet: Break eggs and separate whites and yolks. Place yolks in jar and store in refrigerator for some other use, since they are not an ingredient in this recipe. Melt butter and 1 tablespoon olive oil and add egg whites to a saucepan, preferably an omelet pan with sloping sides. Cook until egg whites have set. Put aside.

To make the filling: Sauté onion and mushrooms in remaining olive oil until mushrooms are cooked but not brown. Place spinach in pan. Add a bit of water if there is not enough liquid to wilt spinach. Add sour cream and stir till mixture holds together.

To serve: Place egg whites on serving dish. Carefully add filling and roll egg white into sausage shape. With sharp knife, cut into circles and tilt each piece to expose the filling. Decorate with chopped tomato.

Bread

Harvest Crackers

MAKES 100 CRACKERS

A gourmet food store sold a wonderful but expensive cracker densely filled with nuts. My friend Gabriel, a talented chef, replicated these crackers, adding her own personal touch. I make these in a large quantity, freeze in batches, then thaw them when I'm having a party. Perfect served with hard or soft cheese. I rarely make my own crackers but this recipe is well worth it; there is nothing as tasty or as healthy for sale in stores.

Equipment: eight mini loaf pans (3 x 5 inches).

2 cups unbleached unenriched white flour
1 teaspoon salt
2 teaspoons baking soda
⅓ cup brown sugar
½ cup pumpkin seeds
¼ cup sunflower seeds
¼ cup flax seeds
1 tablespoon finely chopped rosemary leaves
½ cup currants or golden raisins
⅓ cup honey
⅔ cup buttermilk

To prepare pans: Grease mini loaf pans.

To make the batter: Measure flour, salt, and baking soda into a large mixing bowl and stir to blend. Add brown sugar, seeds, rosemary, and currants. Put honey and but-termilk in small saucepan and melt till they are blended. Add the liquid to the dry ingredients and mix to make a batter. Divide the batter among the small loaf pans.

To bake the crackers: Bake at 325°F for 25–30 minutes. Let loaf pans cool on rack for a couple hours and then remove loaves from their pans. Wrap in airtight bag or aluminum foil and place in refrigerator overnight. (Chilled loaves are easier to cut the next day.) With a sharp knife, cut each loaf into thin slices across the width of the loaf. Place them on cookie sheets in rows. Bake 15 minutes on one side, flip, and bake 10 minutes on the other. Watch carefully since you want to the crackers to be golden and not brown.

Soups

Carrot Soup

SERVES 4

My children loved this soup and it became our traditional Sunday night supper with a cheese soufflé and crunchy bread. It's economical and quick.

Equipment: Food processor or blender

4 tablespoons chopped onion
2 tablespoons butter
3 cups carrots, coarsely chopped
1 quart chicken stock
1 tablespoon tomato paste
2 tablespoons white long-grain rice
½ cup cream or milk

For the garnish:
1 tablespoon butter and finely chopped parsley

To prepare soup: Sauté chopped onions in butter in a heavy-duty saucepan. Add carrots, chicken stock, tomato paste, and rice. Cook until carrots are soft. Puree in food processor till completely smooth or stop while the carrots still have a slightly chunky texture. Add the cream or milk.

To serve: Add a dot of butter on top of each soup bowl and a decorative swirl of chopped parsley.

Sorrel Soup

SERVES 4

Sorrel is appearing more and more frequently in farmers' markets. Sorrel is a cool-season perennial. Though people fawn over the baby leaves when sorrel first appears in the spring, sorrel is still available in the markets into the fall season in the Berkshires and Pioneer Valley. Try this tart and lemony herb with its special zing. Depending on the soil and type of sorrel, the herb can vary in flavor so be sure to adjust this soup recipe to your taste. Introduce friends to sorrel if they haven't tried it. The green color is spectacular.

For the soup:

½ pound butter
2 yellow onions, peeled and thinly sliced
3 garlic cloves, peeled and finely minced
10 cups fresh sorrel leaves, stems removed,
    lightly packed
4 cups chicken stock
3 medium-size white or red potatoes, peeled
    or washed and unpeeled, chopped
¾ cup Italian parsley
1 teaspoon salt
1 teaspoon pepper
2 teaspoons ground nutmeg
½ teaspoon cayenne pepper

For the garnish:

Crème fraîche or Greek-style yogurt
Any colored pepper: red, orange, yellow, or dark green,
    or tomato

To prepare soup: Melt butter in 6-quart saucepan and cook onions and garlic till they are tender, about 5 minutes. Add sorrel, cover and cook until sorrel is wilted, about 5 minutes. Add stock, potatoes, parsley, salt and pepper, nutmeg, and cayenne. Bring to boil. Cook 45 minutes. Put in food processor and puree. Return to saucepan and heat before serving.

To serve: Garnish with crème fraîche or Greek-style yogurt and some finely chopped peppers or tomatoes for color.

Salads

Persimmon and Pomegranate Salad
with Martha's Dressing

SERVES 4

When I visited Japan I was struck by the simplicity of stark trees in the rural countryside with orange persimmons hanging on them. I was young and unfamiliar with this fruit, nor was I very familiar with pomegranates, but both are now available in almost all our grocery stores.

Using orange persimmons, red radicchio lettuce, red pomegranate seeds, and green endive and chicory, this multicolored salad is welcome in the fall when we begin to miss all our lush summer salads. Try this beautiful, colorful salad with "Martha's Salad Dressing."

For the marinade (Martha's Salad Dressing):

1 teaspoon salt
½ teaspoon sugar
½ teaspoon pepper
½ teaspoon paprika
1 clove garlic, crushed
2 tablespoons fresh onion, minced
½ teaspoon dry mustard
½ cup olive oil
¼ cup cider vinegar
½ teaspoon Worcestershire sauce

For the salad:

½ cup pistachios, shelled
½ cup pine nuts
2 Fuyu persimmons (short squatty type), peeled
1 pomegranate, small or medium
2 heads of endive, pulled apart
2 radicchio leaves pulled apart
1 bunch chicory lettuce

To make marinade: Add all Martha's Salad Dressing ingredients to a small jar, place lid on jar and shake. This will make enough marinade for several salads.

To prepare persimmons: Cut persimmons in wedges, put several tablespoons of marinade in dish and marinate persimmons for 2 hours.

To prepare nuts: Heat heavy-bottom fry pan, like a cast-iron pan, and roast nuts for 3–5 minutes. Do not brown.

To prepare pomegranate: Fill sink with enough water to cover pomegranate. Cut pomegranate in half and then submerge under water. Peel skin and membranes away to expose seeds. The seeds will float to surface. Scoop and save them. This method avoids squirting red juices.

To serve: Pull the endive and radicchio leaves apart and toss to mix the red and green leaves. Add some chicory (about one part chicory to two parts radicchio/endive) to create texture. Remove persimmon from marinade, add persimmons to salad and dress lettuce with some marinade. Toss. Decorate with nuts.

Escarole, Apple, Fennel, and Onion Salad with Baby Ginger Dressing

SERVES 4

Our favorite tomato and basil have disappeared with the heat of summer and now it is time to turn to making a salad from fall produce. Escarole is hardy and available through a few frosts, while apples are ubiquitous. It's important to have a mandoline slicer to create the thin slices and rings needed for a beautiful presentation of this salad. A simple model is fine; you don't need the fancy, multiple-blade slicer.

For the salad mixture:

2 apples, very firm, like Braeburn, Empire, Gala, Mitsu
1 large red onion, peeled
1 fennel bulb
½ cup cilantro or mint
1 head escarole, washed and torn into bite-size pieces
¼ cup walnuts, cut in medium-size pieces

For the dressing:

2 tablespoons white wine vinegar
1 teaspoon finely grated lemon and orange zest
1 teaspoon finely grated ginger*
1 teaspoon coarsely ground pepper
3 tablespoons olive oil

Note: Try the young baby ginger available in the fall farmers' markets. If you use a mature, brown ginger, freeze it first. It will grate easier and you won't have to struggle with fibers.

To prepare salad: Cut the apples in half and take out pith and seeds. Hold the apple at an angle and cut thin slices on the mandoline. Perform same motion with a whole onion to produce thin slices. Cut off the stalks of the fennel (save and add to soup or other dish) and, starting with the fat part of the bulb, make thin slices of fennel with the mandoline cutter.

Meanwhile make salad dressing: Mix wine vinegar, lemon and orange zest, ginger, pepper and olive oil together. Whip with fork or put in small bottle and shake. Dress apples, onion, and fennel with the salad dressing.

To serve: Arrange apples, onion, cilantro or mint and fennel on top of escarole. Sprinkle top with walnut pieces and a bit of finely chopped fennel fronds.

Entrees

Spinach Pasta with Roasted Squash and Sage Pesto

SERVES 4

The sage pesto coats the pasta and turns it a shade of green. With the addition of dots of orange squash, this dish makes a lovely, simple fall presentation. As you will learn in this cookbook, pesto sauce is not limited to basil, but can be made of various herbs and vegetables. I chose sage because it grows well into the fall, even surviving frosts in the heart of Massachusetts. Pesto sauces are easy to make, easy to add to a dish to "spice it up," and you won't need to buy them in the store anymore.

For the pasta:

1 fairly large butternut squash

1 pound spinach pasta, fettuccine or rotelli style

3–5 tablespoons pesto sauce, ideally sage (see recipe below)

3 tablespoons Parmesan cheese

For the sage pesto:

2 cups sage leaves

2 cloves garlic

½ cup Parmesan cheese, grated

½ cup chopped walnuts or pine nuts

¾ cup olive oil

Salt and pepper to taste

To prepare the pesto sauce: Place sage leaves, garlic, cheese, and nuts in food processor or blender. Pulse for a few seconds and then—on the puree speed—slowly drip olive oil into the mixture. Puree till well blended. Scrape sides of bowl and use immediately or store in airtight container for few days in refrigerator. Pesto freezes well.

To prepare squash: Peel skin, cut in half, and bake in oven at 375°F for 25–30 minutes till barely soft. Do not let squash become mushy; squash should be slightly firm.

In the meantime: Boil 4 quarts water and cook pasta according to the directions, usually 5–10 minutes till al dente. Drain and toss the pasta with the pesto. Gently fold in the cubes of squash. Sprinkle some Parmesan cheese on top.

Brussels Sprouts with Organic Sausage

SERVES 4

Since brussels sprouts grow well in colder climates like Massachusetts, they are a popular regional fall vegetable. Often the stalk is cut at the base and the whole stalk, with all its little green balls, is sold as a unit. I love carrying the stalks, almost like a bouquet of flowers, in my market basket.

Roasted brussels sprouts with maple syrup are delicious, but the real secret to converting anyone to absolutely loving brussels sprouts is to peel the leaves and lightly sauté them. When my daughter was a teacher in New York City, she learned the trick from Charlie Palmer, the celebrity chef whose twins were in her kindergarten class. Charlie Palmer says all four of his sons adore brussels sprouts prepared this way. Adding sausage creates a one-dish meal.

Food producers in the Berkshire Pioneer Valley region, such as Jeremy Stanton of The Meat Market, are creating European-style organic sausage of chicken, pork, beef, or lamb and vegetables. They are not your salty supermarket sausages, full of additives and who knows what. Buy some and feel good about eating sausage!

4 sausages, such as hot Italian or your preference
2 tablespoons olive oil
15 brussels sprouts, each peeled apart
2 tablespoons balsamic vinegar
Salt
Coarse black pepper

To prepare the brussels sprouts: Peel off the outer leaves of each brussels sprout. You can save the inner pale green core for another dish or cut them in smaller pieces and add to this recipe.

To cook the recipe: Sauté sausage in saucepan till sausage is nicely brown and then set aside. Scrape pan to collect drippings from sausage and add olive oil. Put brussels sprout leaves into pan and sauté quickly. Place sausage back in pan and cook for 1 minute to warm it. Add balsamic vinegar and salt and pepper to taste.

Trout Amandine with Brown Butter

SERVES 4

Freshwater fish is a joy, and there are lots of fishing holes in western and central Massachusetts. Several websites list streams, ponds, and lakes that stock trout. See www.visit-massachusetts .com for fish species and locations where you can put in a boat or rent equipment. If you want to buy rather than catch your own fish, try upscale markets, since most carry good fish. I am impressed, however, with the quality of fish at some of the New England grocery store chains, like Shaws. Here is one of my favorite fish recipes.

1 cup milk or buttermilk

1 cup finely ground cornmeal or ½ corn meal
   and ½ white flour

¼ cup coarsely ground cornmeal (use finely ground
   if unavailable)

10 tablespoons (5 ounces) unsalted butter

3 tablespoons olive oil

2 medium-size (1–2 pounds) fresh trout with head
   and bones

¾ cup thin almond slices, blanched or with skin

2 teaspoons lemon juice

1 lemon, cut into thin slices or wedges

2 teaspoons minced Italian parsley

To coat the trout: Put milk in one shallow dish and cornmeal (all fine or mixture of fine and coarsely ground) and flour in another dish. Dip fish first in milk and then coat with cornmeal. Put aside.

To cook fish: Melt half of the butter with the olive oil in a large saucepan. When frying pan is hot, place whole fish in pan and fry, pressing down on fish to cook center and to brown the coating. Cook about 3–5 minutes on each side. Cut small incision in fattest part of fish and test to see if done. Fish should be flaky and no longer pink. Remove fish from pan.

To make brown butter: Melt the remaining butter in the saucepan, scraping bottom to release the brown scrapings left from cooking the fish. Add the almonds and cook over medium heat, constantly watching as almond slices burn quickly. Add lemon juice.

To serve: Place fish on a serving platter and pour almonds and brown butter sauce over the fish. (Be sure to give each guest some of the almonds and brown butter.) Decorate each trout with thin slices or wedges of lemon scattered around fish. Top fish with minced parsley.

Vegetables en Papillote
(Parchment Package)

SERVES 4

The recipe is long because of the instructions on folding a parchment package, but making the dish is really quite simple. The presentation is impressive and, although it is a vegetarian dish, the vegetables and spices blend in a complex manner. After I visited Aleppo, Syria, in 2010, I began to use Aleppo pepper. It particularly suits this recipe by bringing spice but not the heat of most peppers. Cooking in a parchment packet combines steaming and roasting, and captures moisture and flavor. Once the parchment packages are filled and sealed, you can relax with a glass of wine knowing that each guest will be delighted when she opens her individual serving and the steam and aroma tingle her nose. This is an unusual dish with an element of surprise, like opening a present.

Equipment: Parchment bags

Note: If you can't find parchment bags for this recipe, you can create the holder for the filling from parchment paper, which is available in most supermarkets. (My market advertises them as a "green" alternative to aluminum foil.)

2 cups bulgur

4 cups water

1 lemon, zest and juice

2 tablespoons butter

½ cup chopped onion

2 cloves garlic, peeled and diced

Large bunch thyme, leaves removed from stems

1 teaspoon Aleppo pepper (or equal parts sweet paprika and cayenne pepper)

1 sweet potato, washed

6 medium-size carrots, washed

4–5 tablespoons olive oil

½ pound green beans, cut into 3-inch lengths

¼ cup pecans

15 mushrooms, shiitake or cremini, chopped

2 tablespoons parsley, finely chopped

6 ounces feta cheese

Prepare the bulgur: Usual proportion is 1 cup bulgur to 2 cups water. Boil the water, add bulgur, and cook according to directions (usually 10 minutes). Let stand till bulgur absorbs all water. Drain any excess water.

Prepare butter-lemon sauce: Zest lemon, cut it in half, and squeeze and save juice (discard seeds). Melt 2 tablespoons butter and add onion, garlic, lemon zest and juice of lemon, fresh thyme, and Aleppo pepper and cook for 3 minutes. Add to bulgur.

Prepare the parchment filling: Thinly slice the sweet potato and carrots. Toss them in 2 tablespoons olive oil with the green beans.

Parchment bag: Place ¼ of the bulgur mixture in the bag. Top with ¼ of each vegetable, sweet potato slices, carrots, and green beans. Seal the end by folding over several times. Skip to baking instructions.

Prepare the papillote package (if you do not have the parchment bag): Fold parchment paper and cut 4 heart shapes. The spine of each heart should be 12 inches long and the widest part of the heart should be about 8 inches wide.

To fill the papillote: Put one parchment heart on counter. Place ¼ of bulgur mixture on the fat part of the left side of the heart leaving ¾–1 inch around the edges. Arrange ¼ of each vegetable: sweet potato slices, carrots, and green beans on top of bulgur.

To seal the papillote: Place right side of heart on top of filling on the left side. Seal parchment heart starting at the bottom left side of the heart, pull about 1 inch of the two edges forward and fold down, pressing tightly to seal. Then take another inch of the edges, fold up and seal. Continue all the way around the edges until all the edges are all folded. Place finished parchment heart on cookie sheet or sheet pan. Watch *Bon Appétit* video for a visual demonstration: www.bonappetit.com/test-kitchen/inside -our-kitchen/article/how-to-fold-parchment-paper-to-cook -en-papillote. (**Note:** Now comes my secret, sometimes I seal the edges by hand but I have also been known to use a small stapler if I am in a hurry.) Continue filling and sealing the remaining three parchment packets and place on cookie sheet.

Bake: Roast in 425°F oven for 20 minutes.

Meanwhile, prepare the topping: Toss pecans and mushrooms in remaining olive oil. Using another shelf of the oven, roast pecans for 3 minutes and mushrooms for 6 minutes. Mix with 1–3 tablespoons olive oil and 2 tablespoons chopped parsley. Set aside.

To serve: Place each parchment packet on a plate and open (make an X with scissors or knife) at the table to release the aroma for each person. Pass roasted pecans, mushrooms, and feta cheese mixed together.

Desserts

French Apple Tarte

6–10 SERVINGS DEPENDING ON SIZE OF SLICES.

When a good friend said she couldn't make pie crusts, I suggested she make this French tarte. You just have to roll out one piece of dough, and if you make a small tear, it can be repaired. The dough will be covered by fruit and no one will know. This recipe is truly easy to prepare and makes an impressive aesthetic impact when served. The dough and apples are thin and therefore delicate and tasty. I prefer the tarte served alone, but you may want to serve it with crème fraîche or ice cream.

Equipment: Cookie sheet and pastry brush

For the pie crust:

2 cups flour
1 teaspoon salt
1½ sticks unsalted butter
½ cup water, with ice cubes
¼ cup white sugar

For the fruit:

4–6 baking apples, such as Granny Smith

For the glaze:

1 cup apricot jam (or rose hip jam)
¼ cup water

To make the pie dough: Place flour and salt in a medium-size bowl and add butter, chopping butter into size of peas, using knife in each hand or working it quickly with your fingers. Drip cold water onto flour-butter mixture and gather the mixture till it holds a ball shape and is not sticky. Knead two to four times until flour and butter seem fairly well blended. Chill in refrigerator several hours.

To roll out the pie dough: Sprinkle flour on countertop and roll out the pastry crust into a rectangle shape. Transfer the crust to a cookie sheet. Trim the edges to form a rectangle, 8 x 14 inches. Then cut a ½-inch square out of each corner and wet all the dough edges with water. Fold ½-inch strip of dough—on all sides—over toward center of rectangle to make a "curb" all the way around the rectangle. With a fork (oyster fork is perfect), press down the pastry edges. The fork will seal the edges and create a nice pattern. Gently prick the center of the rectangle of the dough to prevent the dough from buckling when it bakes. Sprinkle the interior with a light layer of sugar.

To prepare the fruit: Peel and cut apples into uniform slices, ⅛- to ¼-inch thick. Either lay the apple slices vertically or horizontally in rows, overlapping the slices. Bake in 400°F oven for 20 minutes or until the edges of the dough are light brown.

To prepare glaze: Melt apricot jam with a little water and whisk with fork until the jam is smooth. Remove tarte from oven when it is nearly cooked and coat apples and dough with apricot glaze. Return to oven and bake until the tarte is a glorious golden color. The tarte is best served warm.

Chocolate Nut Cake with Cherries

12 SERVINGS

My daughter does not like cake and this is the ONLY one she will eat. When she was little, I had to be creative about what to serve for a birthday party since almost all other children DO like cake. I included this recipe when I taught cooking classes to six nationalities while I lived in Sweden. The cake was everyone's favorite. I did not select this cake to be photographed for the book because it always caves in a wee bit in the middle. Still, if you sprinkle the top with powdered sugar, it looks fine and its moist, nutty taste makes it memorable.

Equipment: 9-inch springform pan

4 eggs
2 cups sugar
1 cup white, unbleached flour
½ pound (2 sticks) butter, melted
4 teaspoons cocoa, good quality, unsweetened
2 teaspoons baking powder
1 tablespoon vanilla extract, kirsch, or brandy
1 cup nuts (roasted skinless hazelnuts or walnuts),
   coarsely chopped
12–15 cherries (fresh pitted or canned)
½ cup powdered sugar

To prepare cake pan: Grease a springform pan.

To make the cake: Place eggs in large bowl, whip lightly with fork, add sugar, flour, butter, cocoa, baking powder, vanilla, and the nuts. Stir till blended. Pour into springform pan. Drop cherries into the batter close to the edges.

To bake cake: Bake at 350°F for 45 minutes until knife comes out clean. Cool and then take ring off springform pan.

To serve: Top with powdered sugar, sprinkled through a fine sieve.

Restaurants

Bistro Les Gras

Executive Chef: Daniel Martinez
Northampton

Daniel and Elizabeth Martinez have created a little jewel of a restaurant, Bistro Les Gras. For a young couple, owning and managing their own restaurant, which opened in 2008, is an extraordinary accomplishment. Daniel is the chef and Elizabeth is hostess and business manager. The colors of the restaurant reminded me of the soft orange warmth of an apricot. Wood, art, and simple table settings create an attractive atmosphere where guests come to dine in comfort. Daniel and Elizabeth are fulfilling their dream of establishing a restaurant that brings the excellence of fine cooking techniques to New England ingredients, with a French twist.

Daniel and Elizabeth use the term "hyperlocal" to explain their commitment to using regional foods to bring the farm to the table. The Pioneer Valley is a cornucopia of abundant ingredients, which Daniel utilizes. He shops for the freshest ingredients and incorporates them into a menu that changes almost daily, transforming them into wonderful dining experiences for his customers. Daniel does all the cooking and makes everything in house, from condiments to cured meats.

Daniel experienced interesting geographic contrasts growing up with his immediate family. He was based in cold Minnesota, but luxuriated in warm, sunny New Mexico, where he spent summers with his grandparents. Daniel started in the restaurant industry at an early age. He was just fifteen when he began building his skills by learning nearly every job—serving, bartending, managing, dishwashing—and he finally found his preferred spot as a chef. Daniel was employed at various restaurants in Minnesota, New Mexico, Portland, and Manhattan (including the famous Daniel Restaurant in New York City) and then attended the Institute of Culinary Education (ICE) in Manhattan.

Meanwhile, Elizabeth, who was raised in Northampton, Massachusetts, began her career as a trained chemist. She laughs when she describes her occupation as not being an ideal topic for a cookbook. "I was an analytical chemist focusing on environmental chemistry at a gray-water treatment company in New Mexico. I ran a lab where we created systems that turned wastewater into gray water using a series of biological tanks. It was quite a switch when I married Daniel and became involved in the food business."

Daniel and Elizabeth met in Taos, New Mexico, while they were both working at a restaurant there. After they married, it wasn't long before they put their plans into action and founded their own restaurant. Bistro Les Gras is located just off the central busy hub of Northampton, near the Smith College campus and across from the stately Forbes Library, a historic landmark because of its magnificent Romanesque style and as one of the earliest fireproof buildings in America. The library houses President Calvin Coolidge's papers.

Daniel and Elizabeth told me, "Bistro Les Gras won the lottery. We were, at random, selected to receive a coveted liquor license." This will only enhance their libation offerings. Elizabeth has already assembled a serious wine list, and they plan to continue an annual tradition of hosting a "Cochon" evening, a "wine and swine extravaganza," which features a whole pig from Mockingbird Farm. Another annual event is the restaurant's Locavore Dinner, with dishes based exclusively on local ingredients from within a twenty-five-mile radius.

I asked Daniel and Elizabeth about the name of their restaurant, since it seems to translate literally as "Small Restaurant of Fats." Most people are familiar with Mardi Gras, or "Fat Tuesday," a day associated with celebrations and the last day to eat rich foods before the ritual fasting for forty days of Lent starts on Ash Wednesday. Daniel and Elizabeth dream of someday traveling to the quaint town of Les Gras, in a region of lavender fields in eastern France near the Swiss border. This town was branded on their minds when they searched for a name for their restaurant, and they enjoy the association with Mardi Gras: "the joy of indulging in good food!"

Daniel is sharing his recipe for lobster and pumpkin bisque, which brings the taste of lobster and summer into the fall season by combining it with a bisque of Printemps Rouge squash. This squash has a mellow complexity that makes it stand apart from the more common acorn or butternut squashes. Enjoy creating this recipe yourself or go to dine at Bistro Les Gras, a favorite of local food aficionados and parents of Smith College students who come from all over the country and the world—and delight in finding a refined restaurant in this small college town.

Bisque d'Homard et Citrouille au Curry
(Curried Lobster and Pumpkin Bisque)

SERVES 6

2 lobsters, 1½–2 pounds each

4 bay leaves

2 onions, diced

2 celery stalks, diced

2 leeks (white part only) or 1 medium-size fennel bulb, thinly sliced

½ cup white wine

1 teaspoon white peppercorn

1 teaspoon cardamom pods

1 teaspoon cumin seed

¼ teaspoons mustard seed

1 tablespoon turmeric, ground

Pinch cayenne

4 tablespoons butter

1 medium-size cooking pumpkin, peeled, seeded and chopped (about 1 quart of meat)

½ cup Cognac

½ cup cream

½ cup fresh squeezed lemon juice

Salt to taste

2-inch piece ginger root, finely minced (garnish)

Cilantro (garnish)

Olive oil (garnish)

To prepare the lobsters: Steam lobsters until bright red and cooked through, 15–18 minutes. Pick meat and reserve.

To prepare the stock: Lightly toast the shells in a dry saucepan and let cool. Place shells on a sturdy cutting board, cover with a towel and crush shells with a mallet or hammer until the pieces are fairly small. Place crushed shells, bay leaves, half the onion, half the celery, half the leeks, white wine, and enough water to cover the shells with a ½ inch of water in a large stock pot. Bring to simmer and skim off any foam that arises. Cook for 45 minutes then strain and save liquid.

Meanwhile, while stock is cooking, prepare the spices: Toast peppercorns, cardamom, cumin, and mustard until dark in color and very fragrant. Grind in spice grinder with turmeric and cayenne and reserve.

To cook the pumpkin: Place remaining leek, onion, celery, and butter in the saucepan and cover with water. Cook over moderate heat until all vegetables soften. Add pumpkin and spice blend to pot, cook for 2 minutes and add Cognac and reduce by half. Add enough reserved lobster broth to cover pumpkin by an inch and simmer until pumpkin is falling-apart soft, adding more broth (or water) as you go if needed.

To finish pureed soup: Place pumpkin and liquid stock in a food processor or blender and stir in cream and lemon juice. If soup is too thick, add a little lobster broth or water to thin out. Season well with salt.

To serve: Garnish with reserved lobster meat, grated fresh ginger, thinly sliced celery, celery leaves, cilantro, and olive oil.

Trattoria Rustica

Owner and Executive Chef: Davide Manzo
Pittsfield

Just to prove that America is a melting pot, you will find the flavors of Pompeii, Italy, in the western Massachusetts city of Pittsfield. As you open the heavy wooden door with cast-iron hinges and studs, you enter a Pompeiian world created by Davide Manzo, the owner and chef of Trattoria Rustica.

Davide was fascinated with the history and culture of his hometown, a sophisticated city with a tragic story. Pompeii was buried in volcanic ash in 79 BC, preserving the structures, mosaics, and even the bodies of people for over 1,500 years until the city was uncovered. He loved the myths of Greek and Roman gods almost as much as food, which was central to Italian life. Davide was exposed to fine cooking at an early age, as his grandparents owned a trattoria on the Amalfi Coast. Later he worked with his mother and sister in an Italian restaurant, but his dream was always to open his own. As I interviewed food producers, they often spoke of their dream, not just falling into some career path but having a driving ambition to fulfill a vision of what they wanted to do or be in life. It is obvious that passion drives many of those who work with food, and Davide is no exception. He finally opened his own restaurant, but it involved literally building the space by hand.

When you visit the trattoria, ask Chef Manzo to share his scrapbook with you. Pictures chronicle the transformation of a "ruin," a bare, abandoned space in the bottom of a building in downtown Pittsfield. The ceiling was a mess, and the floor was dirt. Davide, who had worked in construction for many years after he came to the United States in 1970, began the hard work of making his ideal space, one infused with atmosphere and materials evoking his hometown of Pompeii, near present-day Naples. Now the ceiling is covered with warm wood, which creates a

cozy atmosphere. The floors are tiled. In an unused space behind the restaurant's building, Davide built a terrace for dining alfresco in warm weather. He designed the accessibility ramp in such a way that the restaurant was able to add some tables for two on a raised platform. He also added personal touches, like oil lamps that resemble ancient Roman lanterns and furniture he welded with a friend.

At the core of this restaurant is the burning "heart" of the Pompeiian-style oven Davide built singlehandedly with specific Pompeiian tiles he carried from Italy. Although he knew exactly how the traditional oven should be built, the Massachusetts building regulations required him to follow a slightly different pattern. After the restaurant opened, there was a fire in the oven. Though it closed the restaurant for a while, the fire convinced the fire marshals that Davide was more of an expert on Italian ovens than they, and they let him rebuild the oven in the true Pompeiian form.

The oven is where you will find Chef Manzo, if he isn't circulating and talking to guests. He lovingly bakes all the restaurant's bread in his oven and all of the wood-fired oven dishes, from a succulent chop to a special fish he has flown in from Italy. It takes a master to build the oven to the right temperature, control the heat, and properly cook each dish. You won't be disappointed. I had the best veal chop I have ever eaten in my life—slightly pink and infused with the smoky flavors of the wood. Davide says his oven produces "an ancient flavor that cannot be duplicated in a modern oven or stovetop," and that he is "living my dream, to prove to people that the flavors are there in the fire. If you go to the ruins at Pompeii, you will see ovens similar to mine."

The aesthetics, the food, and the candles all add to the romantic atmosphere, but it is Chef Manzo himself who creates his own charisma. He talks with customers, sharing his love of his food, wine, and his culinary tradition. He told me when I visited that he had invited all of his staff

to go to his house that day to participate in making wine. "Of course, I can't sell the wine. I only wanted to share the process with the staff, for them to smell the aroma and feel the texture of the grapes. As they work in the restaurant, I want them to have a special appreciation of the role of wine and become knowledgeable about the wines we sell." This is a man who goes beyond the ordinary. He lives his traditions, and his staff and customers are family.

I suggest you experience the romantic atmosphere of Trattoria Rustica, Chef Manzo's generous spirit, and the excellent, simple, authentic foods of *la cucina napoletana*. The restaurant is a gift to the city of Pittsfield.

Linguine con Vongole

SERVES 4

Thin pasta with clams is especially popular in southern Italy, thus it is a logical recipe to appear on Chef Davide Manzo's menu at Trattoria Rustica. It's deceptively simple and creates a light pasta dish for a fall evening. Clams, like other fresh seafood, are being imported from the east coast of Massachusetts to the central and western regions by such fishmongers as Berkfish.

1 pound best quality linguine pasta

8 garlic cloves, chopped extremely fine

4 cups cherry tomatoes

1 cup olive oil

2 pounds littleneck clams

2 cups dry white wine

Water as needed

Black pepper to taste

Italian parsley as garnish

To prepare the pasta: Boil 4 quarts of water and cook pasta per package directions, usually 10–12 minutes until al dente.

To prepare the sauce: Sauté garlic and cherry tomatoes in olive oil in a large skillet until tomatoes are tender. Note: Be careful to not brown or overcook. Add the clams and white wine. Cover and steam until clams open. Add bit of water if you sense there is not enough liquid in the pan. Be sure to discard any clams that don't open.

To serve: Divide linguine among four wide bowls and top each with clams and sauce, divided evenly. Sprinkle top with coarse black pepper and garnish with some Italian parsley.

Food Producers

Pierce Brothers Coffee

Owners: Sean and Darren Pierce
Greenfield

The deep, rich color of the freshly roasted coffee is enticing and the upbeat attitude of brothers Sean and Darren is contagious. I wasn't sure if I was high on the wonderful cup of coffee the brothers offered me or the brothers' outgoing, friendly nature. I met the brothers, Sean and Darren Pierce, in a spacious brick structure in Greenfield, Massachusetts, a former shoe factory, which they have repurposed to serve as the roasting facility, offices, warehouse, and headquarters for their wholesale coffee business, Pierce Brothers Coffee.

I was eager to meet Sean and Darren and see their operation, especially to learn the key to their success at being a medium-size coffee business in the heart of Massachusetts, holding its own against some of the biggest international conglomerates in the world. One of the most exciting features of their business model is that the Pierce Brothers air-roast their coffee. With the air-roasted method, the coffee beans are propelled into the air and roasted like popcorn

without touching each other. This hot-air convection method roasts the coffee more evenly and consistently than the traditional drum roasting method, which can cause the beans to stick to the drum and develop a bitter, burned taste. With an air-roasting technique, the beans are roasted at a higher temperature, which results in the chaff being completely burned off the bean. With the drum method, often some of the chaff will stick and roast onto the coffee bean. The Pierce brothers explain, "When you see a ring in the bottom of your coffee cup, it is from the soot from the chaff." The brothers like to say that their roasting method results in "The Clean Bean"—a "clarity of flavor" that allows the genuine taste of the roasted bean to shine through.

It is pretty wild to watch the beans popping around and then pouring, glistening, out of the hot machine. It would make sense that everyone in the world would use this coffee-roasting method, yet the problem is that the man who invented the roasting machine, Michael Sivetts, is no longer alive. The brothers owned one of his machines but to obtain a larger oven, they were forced to purchase one of his old machines and rehab it into a size that now handles their increased volume of business.

Their unique roasting method wouldn't be enough to set them apart. Their success is built on their drive, work ethic, sacrifices, and sweat equity. As they prepared to launch their business, they sometimes worked as many as three jobs. The brothers started the company in the basement of their parents' house, where they worked and lived. For years they built up credit on their credit cards and, Sean says, "One day we spent nearly $2,000 on a single piece of machinery. From that day, there was no going back. We were in the coffee business." Ironically, dreaming big and being naïve were also assets. Darren recalled a savvy businessman who took him aside and asked how he planned to start a company on credit, pay back the interest, *and* make enough profit to grow his business. Darren hadn't really thought of that.

Both brothers acknowledge that they are told over and over by customers that they are chosen over "the big guys" because of their service. The Pierce brothers and their team are totally dependable. Darren comments, "To say that it takes a village is such a cliché, but in our case it is true. We built the business as brothers with the help of our family. Now we are building a community business by hiring people needing a good job and a career path. Summer workers come back after they graduate from school and get promoted. We liked one young man and offered him a job driving our delivery truck. The only problem was that he didn't know how to drive. We were a bit stunned, but told him, 'Never mind; we'll find you a job.' We trained him and he is now our chief coffee roaster—one of the most critically important jobs in our business."

As the brothers learned more about the complexities of coffee roasting and the manner of growing and supporting the farmers who grow the coffee, they traveled to some of the countries that grow the coffee they purchase. The brothers have bought coffee in Costa Rica, Nicaragua, and Peru. Sean has traveled mainly to Mexico and Guatemala and, for the first time, the brothers will go to Sumatra this year. As they developed bonds with their growers and their families, they sought out fair trade, organic coffee sources that offer fair purchasing prices to the farmer. Having a chance to meet and interact directly with the cooperatives, the brothers came to fully appreciate how critical these cooperatives are to farmers and their families. The fair trade cooperatives teach farmers how to rotate their crops to ensure sustainable practices or, for example, to raise bees for the benefit of the coffee. The farmers can share resources, such as collectively building a concrete patio where they can dry their coffee. No one farmer can afford such a resource, but together they can provide important infrastructures. Sean and Darren appreciate knowing that the farmers are proud of their work and building a tangible and valuable business to pass on to their children. Darren says working with fair trade cooperatives was almost easier than obtaining US certification for organic coffee. Certification requires that not only is the coffee grown under strict organic conditions, every bag of beans is traced and recorded, and the factory building and employees must comply with all the strict organic conditions.

The brothers certainly charmed me. They aren't the in-your-face boasting type, but their genuine passion and pleasure in their growing success of the business is infectious. They grin when they talk about their most popular brand and the name they created for it, Fogbuster. "Isn't that just the coolest—a coffee that breaks through that morning haze and gets you going?"

By the time I left my visit at Pierce Brothers Coffee I had become an enthusiastic supporter of and cheerleader for their business. Pierce Brothers Coffee has gained a niche in the coffee market with the quality of their service to customers. Located in what is called the Five College Region, the brothers are providing coffee to many of the local colleges as well as other venues in New England. These are big accounts for a medium-size family business. One popular item that is starting to take off is a concentrated, cold-brewed coffee that comes in a large container. You turn a spout and add coffee to a glass of ice and, "Voilà, it's ice coffee." Another popular offering is the Pierce Brothers "Coffees from Around the World," a different coffee each month for six months. An innovative new item is their Pierce Brothers Coffee Rub. It took the brothers two years to get the right mixture of spices and ingredients.

It contains Pierce Brothers Fogbuster coffee, cocoa powder for a touch of chocolate taste, standard flavors like sea salt, pepper, garlic, and onion, but it is the lively addition of mustard, coriander, dill seed, mesquite, cumin, and celery that makes this rub sing. Look for it at stores selling Pierce Brothers Coffee beans and rub some on a skirt steak or chicken. I've brushed the rub on vegetables before grilling them. Adds a great punch to what might have been average-tasting grilled zucchini slices. Order the Pierce Brothers Coffee Rub or their coffees online at www.piercebroscoffee.com. While you are waiting for their rub to arrive, you can try the following recipe for your own coffee rub.

Coffee Rub

MAKES 2 OUNCES

The basics:

1 tablespoon espresso grind of a quality coffee

2 tablespoons chile powder

1 tablespoon light brown sugar

1 tablespoon black pepper, preferably coarse ground

Optional:

½ teaspoon cayenne powder

1½ teaspoons paprika

½ teaspoon cumin

To make the rub: Mix all ingredients in a small bowl.

To apply the rub: Use hands to rub onto food or add enough olive oil (½ cup) to make a liquid spread and then apply the rub, using a pastry or basting brush, to meat, fish, or vegetables.

Note: You can let the spice soak in for a while or cook your food right away. The spice radiates even without marinating.

Hungry Ghost Bread

Jonathan Stevens and Cheryl Maffie
Northampton

Just the name gives this place an interesting vibe. After all, the site had a previous life as a hideout for the Secret Service, which holed up there with hotlines when President Nixon went to visit his daughter Julie at her Smith College dormitory across the street. Some of the odds and ends of the wiring are still in place. The ghost of Nixon is gone by now, as are the Northampton Chamber of Commerce and chiropractor offices that were once here, before it was converted to a bakery where the new ghost lives. The term "Hungry Ghost" in Buddhist lore refers to people who were so greedy in their previous lives that they are eternally afflicted with an insatiable hunger. Owners Jonathan Stevens and Cheryl Maffie named the bakery after their sourdough starter, whose voracious appetite required them to feed it twice daily.

This sourdough starter is at the core of the excellence of the breads at Hungry Ghost. Master Baker Jonathan only produces breads made from a natural starter, which demands close attention. The starter is a live organism—a mixture of wild yeast and bacteria that converts flour, water, and a touch of salt into spectacular loaves of bread with complex inner flavor and crunchy outer crusts.

Sourdough breads are demanding to create. Though they need to be fermented longer, the results are worth the extra investment of time because the fermentation adds a special flavor and nutritive richness to the bread. Plus the high water content in the dough—which makes it tricky to handle—has the positive effect of helping to neutralize the phytates in flour that interfere with absorption, making the gluten in flour more digestible. Hungry Ghost's breads are healthier and more easily digested than traditional wheat breads. Jonathan likes to remind his customers that not all sourdough breads have a sour taste; in fact, some have a mild flavor. What is consistently true for sourdough bread is their better flavor and texture and longer shelf life.

Jonathan brings a Zen-like focus to his bread baking. He doesn't fool around with rolls or a wide variety of bread types and styles. The bakery doesn't even bother to sell coffee. "There are plenty of coffee places nearby," Jonathan points out. "I prefer to focus on a select repertoire of the finest quality breads using heritage grains and baked in my wood-burning oven."

In his insatiable desire to bake the "best bread ever," Jonathan has built and baked in several ovens. Now he proudly cooks bread in a Llopis oven, which is pretty sexy. It has a red heart: The firebox glows from the wood burning. This Spanish oven is a combination masonry and wood-fired treasure with an amazing rotating floor that turns to provide easy access for moving bread loaves in and out of the oven. It took five weeks to assemble and bakes bread and pizza equally well. Wednesday through Sunday nights, Hungry Ghost offers take-out pizza.

Hungry Ghost first came to my attention because of its efforts to raise consciousness in the Pioneer Valley about the loss of access to the original strains of local wheat, which was an important crop in the Northeast in the nineteenth century. When Jonathan established Hungry Ghost in 2004, he wanted to source all his ingredients locally, especially the most important one, his grains. A call to the Massachusetts Department of Agriculture drew a laugh. As a result, Jonathan and Cheryl put out a challenge to their customers to grow wheat. "After all, it's a grass," they told them. Jonathan planted a few types of grain in the bakery's small front yard as a pilot project. The subsequent effort of 150 Hungry Ghost customers to grow indigenous wheat rather than importing it from the West and Midwest was such a wild idea that it attracted lots of media attention.

Now several farmers provide the bakery with locally sourced grains that haven't been genetically altered and diluted for bulk commercial growing by large agribusinesses. Farmer Gene L'Etoile delivered sacks of grain while I was interviewing Jonathan. He came with his grandson, who was given a chocolate-chip cookie from the bakery. Gene L'Etoile had been farming for thirty years before his two sons joined the business and urged him to diversify into heritage grains. The L'Etoiles' Four Star Farm planted one hundred acres in 2008 and now provides Hungry Ghost with all their whole wheat (Zorro and Glen varieties), rye, a heritage grain called spelt, heirloom corn flour, and a special wheat pastry flour. Growing and processing heritage grains is a delicate, demanding operation, and it was a tough learning curve for both the farmer and the baker. The moisture and protein in heritage grains changes from variety to variety, presenting Jonathan with a challenge with each new batch. If the taste and nutritional value of the grains weren't superior, both he and the growers would have given up.

Fortunately, customers' palates are responding to the rich taste of the heritage grains, the sourdough starter, and the quality of Jonathan's baking in the wood fired oven. Although Hungry Ghost's bread prices are in line with those of other artisanal bakeries, really fine-tasting bread has a cost. Normally a 50-pound bag of wheat costs between $30 and $40, while heritage grains usually run $87.50 a bag. Hungry Ghost sells about two thousand loaves a week in the bakery and through Community Sustained Agriculture (CSA) subscriptions.

Jonathan Stevens can certainly claim to be a master baker now that his breads have been nominated for James Beard awards four times. His past is full of his multitalented roles as carpenter, songwriter, restorer of old houses, puppeteer, stay-at-home dad baking Tassajara cookbook breads, and poet. With humor, Jonathan comments that some people think that Hungry Ghost is only an elaborate front for a vanity press. Check out the bakery's website and you will find examples of Jonathan's poetry (and mention of partner Cheryl's art and daughter Ana's roles in the theater). Try reading "Game in the Rain on the Moon" or my favorite, "St. Dominic's Preview," about a Vulcan pagan bread mixer and Van the Man's music. Of Jonathan's many callings, at the top of the list is being an excellent baker. He is assisted on the business side by his partner Cheryl and daughter Ana, as well as daughter Nia, who bakes bread with her dad.

A bread-baking revolution is occurring in America, surpassing the quality of much of the baking in traditional places like France or northern Europe. The Pioneer Valley is one of the leaders in this movement. Just visit Hungry Ghost and you will witness and taste this revolution.

French and Savory Folds

MAKES APPROXIMATELY 8 FOLDS

Start with some dough. Jonathan saves overproofed or imperfect dough from the bakery and turns it into Savory Folds with yummy fillings. These little packets of goodies are so popular, Jonathan sometimes has to cut into his regular dough supply in order to make enough.

The best dough is made with sourdough and I urge you to cultivate your own sourdough starter. It's simple because wild yeast is floating everywhere. Research the Internet or look in my bread-baking cookbook, *Knead It.* If you don't have the time now, start with easy overnight, high-hydration dough.

For the dough (makes 2 pounds):

1½ cups whole-wheat flour
1½ cups unbleached white flour
¼ teaspoon instant yeast
1¼ teaspoons salt
2 cups of water

Filling for French Fold:

3 tablespoons finely chopped sage
12 dried apricots

Filling for Savory Fold:

2 tablespoons chopped basil
2 tablespoons chopped onion
½ pound extra-sharp cheddar cheese
1 cup sun-dried tomatoes
1 cup chopped mushrooms, like cremini

To make the dough: Place flour, yeast, and salt in bowl. Pour water in and mix until the ingredients hold together. Add some more water till the dough is sticky and a bit gooey. Cover and place in refrigerator overnight.

Continue the next day: Take dough from refrigerator and fold dough several times in letter folds, the way you would fold a letter-size piece of paper for a business envelope. Take the right side and fold ⅔ of the way over. Then cover with the left side. Continue one more time. Let the dough rest until you are ready to make the Savory Folds.

To create exterior of folds: Divide dough in half and roll out dough into large rectangle. Texture dough by poking lightly with a fork to perforate surface. Cut into approximately four squares depending on size of fold you desire. Repeat rolling and cutting of dough.

To prepare filling for French Fold: Sprinkle the sage over the top half of the dough, leaving a ½-inch border around the sides of the top. Cover the sage with apricots placed next to each other, or overlapping slightly. Wet the edges of the dough. Fold the bottom half of the dough over the filling and seal the edges with your fingers or the tines of a fork.

To prepare filling for Savory Fold: Sprinkle chopped basil and onion over the top half of the dough as above. Add a fairly thick slice of cheese. Then add the sun-dried tomatoes and mushrooms. Fold bottom half of dough over the filling and firmly seal with the tines of a fork. (This filling oozes more than the French Fold.)

To bake: Place on cookie sheet and bake at 400°F for 35 minutes.

34   The Berkshires Cookbook

Farm Recipes

Greens Pasta Pie

SERVES 8

Indian Line Farm, South Egremont

Indian Line Farm, one of the first CSAs in America, donated this farm recipe. Look at information about this historic farm on the Fall Tour. Greens abound in the fall farmers' markets because they tolerate cold weather. Greens are inexpensive and loaded with tons of good stuff for us. Those greens in the *Brassica* family (kale, collard, cauliflower, collard greens and brussels sprouts) are known to have anticancer properties. The following recipe makes for a terrific dish to bring to a potluck—everyone will be surprised that greens can taste this good—or to serve at home with soup and bread on a cold evening.

6 ounces thin pasta, like vermicelli or angel hair

2 tablespoons soft or melted butter

⅓ cup Parmesan cheese

5 eggs

2 cups greens (kale, collard, mustard, chard)

2 teaspoons olive oil

1 small onion, chopped

1 cup shredded mozzarella

⅓ cup milk

¼ teaspoon pepper

⅛ tsp nutmeg

½ teaspoon salt

Prepare the pasta: Cook pasta in 4 quarts boiling, salted water according to directions on the package, till al dente, usually about 10–12 minutes. Drain and stir butter, half of the Parmesan cheese, and two beaten eggs into pasta and place in bottom of pie pan. Bake 10 minutes covered with aluminum foil.

Meanwhile, prepare the greens: Remove any hard stems from the greens and chop the leaves coarsely. Heat olive oil and sauté onion and then add greens. Cook until greens are wilted. Add three beaten eggs, mozzarella, milk, and seasonings.

Assemble: Once the pasta mixture is cooked, take it out of the oven, remove aluminum foil, and top with the greens mixture. Sprinkle surface with remaining Parmesan cheese.

Bake: Replace the foil and bake for 35 minutes; uncover and bake for 5 minutes longer, or until cheese is golden brown (or put quickly under broiler).

To serve: Let stand 10 minutes to cool before slicing.

Squash with Herb Cider Glaze

SERVES 4

Farm Girl Farm, Sheffield
Owner: Laura Meister

Farm Girl Farm, founded by Laura Meister, is a small three-acre farm that manages to feed seventy-five CSA members. Laura dreamed of starting a CSA farm with "blind insanity," which she says was the "blindfold she needed for such a crazy plan," but today, with the help of farmgirls and farmboys and bartering for services (including her leased land), Laura is a successful farmer. She is an inspiration to young farmers starting out who don't own land or heavy equipment. Laura has shown them these aren't roadblocks to operating a farm.

2 pounds squash, delicata or other firm winter squash

1½ cups fresh unfiltered apple cider or juice

1 cup water

2 teaspoons sherry vinegar

1 teaspoon salt

Freshly ground black pepper

3 tablespoons unsalted butter

¼ cup very coarsely chopped fresh chives

1 tablespoon coarsely chopped fresh rosemary, sage, or other herb

To prepare the squash: Peel squash with vegetable peeler or knife. Cut in half lengthwise and scrape out the seeds with a spoon. Cut each piece lengthwise in half again and into ½-inch-thick slices.

To cook the squash: Add the squash to a skillet, then the apple cider, water, vinegar, and salt. Cook, stirring occasionally, over medium heat at an even boil until the cider has boiled down to a glaze and the squash is tender, 20–30 minutes. Taste and season with pepper and additional salt if needed.

To make the herb butter: Melt butter in a large pan over low heat and add the herbs. Cook the herbs, stirring, until the butter just begins to turn golden brown, 3–5 minutes. Do not brown the herbs. Cooking the herbs in butter mellows their flavor and improves their texture.

To serve: Place squash in serving dish and pour herb butter over squash.

Lavinia's English Apple Custard Tart

SERVES 8

Clarkdale Fruit Farm, Deerfield

Clarkdale Fruit Farm is a fourth generation farm. Established by a great grandfather who was a gentleman farmer and physician, the farm is now run by Dave Clarkdale and his son Ben. They use only local employees and almost all the work is done by hand, such as the sorting of the apples into wooden crates, not cardboard boxes. This is a recipe contributed by the mother of one of their longtime employees, a fruit picker.

Equipment: 8–9 inch pie pan, buttered

For the pie crust:

1½ cups unbleached white flour
½ teaspoon salt
4 tablespoons unsalted cold butter, chopped into small
    pieces
⅓ cup cold water with ice cubes

For the pie filling:

5–6 apples, such as Baldwin or Northern Spy
½ cup water, depending on moisture of apples
½ cup sugar

For the pie topping:

½ cup butter
½ cup sugar
1 egg yolk
2 whole eggs
1 teaspoon grated lemon rind
Juice from half a lemon
1 teaspoon ground nutmeg

To make the pie crust: Preheat oven to 350°F and place flour and salt in a medium-size bowl. Add butter and cut into size of peas, using two knives in a crisscrossing action—one in each hand or break up the butter into the flour with your hands. Drop cold water onto flour-butter mixture until mixture holds a ball shape and is not sticky. Knead two to four times until flour and butter are well blended. Chill in refrigerator several hours.

To roll out the pie dough: Sprinkle a light dusting of flour on a countertop and roll out the pastry crust 1 inch larger than a 9-inch pie pan. Fold the dough in half and place in buttered pie plate and unfold. Trim the edges of the pie dough to allow a ¾-inch overhang over pie pan. Turn the edge of the crust under. Seal the edges by making pinches every 1½ inches or pressing lightly with a fork around the edges of the pie crust.

To prepare the pie filling: Peel and cut apples into fairly thick slices. Place apples in saucepan with ½ cup water and cook till al dente—firm but not mushy. Drain off almost all liquid and place apple slices in shell. Sprinkle with ½ cup sugar.

To make the filling: Cream together in electric mixer butter, sugar, egg yolk, whole eggs, lemon rind, lemon juice, and nutmeg. Spread mixture over apples. Don't worry if mixture looks curdled; it's supposed to look that way.

To bake: Place in oven at 350°F for 45 minutes or until done. Cool on rack before serving.

FALL TOUR

Fall is magnificent in the Berkshires and Pioneer Valley. The leaf colors are rich yellows and oranges, the fall skies are mostly clear blues, and the grass stays green until the heavy frosts come, usually in late November. Tourist opportunities, especially around food, continually expand and there are a multitude of food spots to explore and lots of cultural offerings. The list below can easily fill your weekend.

Berkshire Farmers' Market, Great Barrington

A wonderful farmers' market situated at the former railroad station in Great Barrington. Wide range of vegetables (including mushrooms), bread, cheeses. Farmers' markets are so wildly popular that Berkshire farmers have organized a fall Holiday Market for customers wanting to buy great farm produce for their Thanksgiving tables. Check out the market the Saturday before Thanksgiving in Great Barrington at Monument Valley Middle School on Monument Valley Road, or on Sunday in Williamstown at the Williams College Towne Field House on Latham Street.

Rubiner's Cheesemongers and Grocers, Great Barrington

While you are in town, stop at Rubiner's, where Matthew Rubiner demonstrates his talents as an impeccable cheesemonger who searches for the very best cheese specimens (domestic or international) and delivers them to you, his customers. This guy is SERIOUS about cheese, which he says he "curates" in order to assemble the finest cheese "exhibition." Let him teach and preach to you. Then go to the cafe to try a grilled cheese sandwich like my favorite: alpine cheese with cornichons and mustard on Pullman white. A new addition is the fishmongering service. Order on Wednesday and you can pick up fresh ocean fish direct from Browne Trading in Portland, Maine, on Friday or Saturday at Rubiner's. Finally, ocean fish in the Berkshires.

Berkshire Mountain Bakery, Housatonic

Follow the Housatonic River out of Great Barrington and stop at Berkshire Mountain Bakery, where Master Baker Richard Bourdon has been making artisanal sourdough bread for twenty-five years in a handsome brick building, formerly a factory. Try one of Richard's famous pizzas—thin sourdough hand-shaped crusts with delicate toppings.

FALL TOUR

Bartlett's Orchard, Richman

Pick apples and eat their to-die-for cider doughnuts.

Harvest Festival for Berkshire Botanical Gardens, Lenox

Check the Internet for the October weekend dates for this annual event supporting one of America's oldest botanical gardens. Food vendors and food products, large farmers' market, local coffee roasters, auction, used books, demonstrations (with animals), tag sale, plants for sale, crafts, and children's activities. This is a quality festival with serious purchasing opportunities.

Berkshire Grown, Fall Fund-raising Dinner, Great Barrington

Berkshire Grown—a large network of regional farmers, food producers, retail food stores and food activists—holds an October fund-raiser hosted by nearly every farmer and chef in the region. Last year the extensive tasting menu included sixty food plates cooked by twenty chefs who each created three items. Of course the chefs of the Red Lion Inn and Old Inn on the Green actively participated.

The Sheffield Store, Sheffield

A hidden gem that locals and vacation-home owners like to keep to themselves, in hopes that this simple cafe won't become crowded with weekend trippers from New York City. Co-owners of the Old Inn on the Green opened this venue to highlight wonderful pastries, gelato, and even a midweek Mexican menu when the chef makes Oaxacan food, a local secret.

Good Dogs Farm, Sheffield

"Honest Dirt, Honest Hands, Honest Food" Roberto Flores jettisoned a career as the innkeeper of Seven Hills Inn, a sixty-room iconic hotel next to Edith Wharton's home, The Mount, for a career in farming. His prior agricultural experience was limited to mowing neighbors' lawns, but with the help of his partner and friends he is now growing a full range of vegetables. You can find his produce at the Sheffield's Farmers' Market on Friday from 3:30–6:30 and featured at many regional restaurants.

Big Elm Brewery, 65 Silver Street, Sheffield

It might be a small town but Sheffield has great things going on. Stop in for free Tours and Tastings Saturday and Sunday, 12:00–4:00 pm. A local couple, Christine and Bill Heaton, sold their brewpub in Pittsfield, to concentrate on just brewing beer (eliminating the food services, which didn't interest them), and now they produce four outstanding locally brewed beers: a great IPA, farmhouse Belgian ale, Gerry Dog Stout beer, and a golden American lager.

Indian Line Farm, South Egremont

Indian Line Farm was founded in 1985 as one of the first Community Supported Agriculture (CSA) farms in the US. Now there are thousands of CSA farms across America. When the farm's owner died suddenly at age forty-nine, the future of the farm was in peril. Miraculously, collaboration between a local community land trust and The Nature Conservancy—utilizing a model legal document developed by the E.F. Schumacher Society for the long-term leasing of farmland—allowed the farm to survive and flourish. If you call ahead (413-528-8301) you can visit this famous farm and enjoy the spectacular fall foliage in the protected lands surrounding the farm.

FALL TOUR

Clarkdale Fruit Farms, Deerfield

Visit this fourth-generation farm and breathe in the stunning views of orchards on rolling hills. Heritage species of apples are enjoying a comeback and buyers are more selective in wanting great-tasting apples, of which Clarkdale has a wide and spectacular selection. My favorite is Northern Spy. I also purchased quince at their farm store. The cider house, near the farm stand, produces a tasty and remarkable pear cider and apple ciders from numerous varieties of apples. The cider is not heated and pasteurized, which allows it to keep its flavor. It won't keep forever, but that's not a problem since I find the cider disappears on the day I buy it. Apples are part of the heritage of this region and now are even more fully appreciated. A special festival is organized to feature, honor, and celebrate apples the first weekend of November. The location varies but the festival is widely advertised, so you can't miss it.

Berkshire Organics, Dalton

Want to pick up an organic, free-range turkey when you are in the region? E-mail or phone order your turkey or your entire Thanksgiving dinner from Berkshire Organics (www.berkshireorganics.com). Ask for a turkey from Nichols Farm in Hancock, Massachusetts. Store open seven days a week, 9:00 am–7:00 pm.

Hungry Ghost Bread, Northampton

When you are on your fall "leaf peeping" trip through the Berkshires and Pioneer Valley, be sure to stop in the college town of Northampton to sample breads, pastries, and pizza at the Hungry Ghost. For four years in a row this bakery has been nominated for a James Beard award. Owners Jonathan Stevens and Cheryl Maffei and daughters operate a bakery that turns out truly exceptional bread: all the regular types of wheat breads with blistery crusts and open crumb, plus ancient grain Kamut bread, spelt with chamomile, and semolina with fennel.

Pierce Brothers Coffee at The Roadside Cafe, Belchertown

Read the story about the Pierce Brothers and check out their new website (www.piercebroscoffee.com) to find the multiple places where you can buy or drink their coffee in the region, such as at The Roadside Cafe, 176 Federal St., Belchertown, a funky breakfast place famous for giant pancakes.

Pioneer Valley Farm and Vineyard, Hatfield

Sixth-generation farmer Casey Burt and his family have expanded their farm operation into growing grapes and making wine. The tasting room was designed to allow you to see (and tour) their entire operation. Though they carry ten varieties such as a red Frontenac and white Cayuga wine, you should try their fruit wines from local Pioneer Valley fruits like blueberry, tomato, and cranberry. The tasting room is open every weekend, October–December, 12:00–5:00 pm. You can taste wines and see their entire operation.

Bistro Les Gras, Northampton

A small restaurant near the center of Northampton is owned by a young couple, Daniel (chef) and Elizabeth (hostess/manager) Martinez. They describe their food as "hyperlocal" and try to buy most ingredients within a small radius of the restaurant. Daniel prepares everything himself, from the condiments to the cured meats. The restaurant recently won a coveted liquor license and you will find all sorts of wonderful libations—and a good wine cellar.

Trattoria Rustica, Pittsfield

Chef and owner Davide Manzo has created a Pompeiian world in the middle of downtown Pittsfield. Open the restaurant's heavy wooden door with cast-iron hinges and decorative markings and you will enter another world. The key to the uniqueness of the restaurant is the wood-burning oven, where Chef Davide makes his own bread and cooks many of the best restaurant dishes.

Winter

Small Plate

Quince "Cheese"

SERVES 20

Quince cheese was a specialty in 18th Century New England, and I hope you will help revive the tradition by making it. You or your friends might know quince cheese from visiting Spain, South America, or Mexico, where it's called *membrillo*. Quince "paste" is a traditional French food served at Christmastime and is very common in Italy. Revive this wonderful fruit paste, once a favorite in America. Wrap a piece and give it as a gift.

Look for quince at your fall farmers' market. The fruit is a cross between a pear and apple, with a knobby surface and a sweet, floral, slightly astringent smell. Most varieties are too hard and sour to eat raw but are perfect to stew, roast, or make into jams. I bought some at Clarkdale Fruit Farms in Deerfield (mentioned in Fall Tour) and the smell of them in the car was intoxicating.

No matter how much I love to cook, time always, always interferes. So when I invite friends or family to a special dinner I am always looking for a way to enhance the meal with something glorious and not hugely complicated. I recommend you make a quantity of quince cheese—it's called a cheese, but it is really a paste/concentrate. Use it as a highlight for entertaining, particularly since it is versatile and impressive combined with your favorite cheese or served with roasted meat or baked into a dessert. Quince cooks to a glorious reddish-orange color and, as the light shines through it, there really isn't any prettier fruit. Enjoy. I've really got you covered with this fruit—you will receive lots of questions and compliments! Spread the word.

Equipment: Food mill (optional), wax paper, large pan like jelly roll or 9 x 13-inch lasagna-style pan

10 pounds of quince (12–15 total)
1 vanilla bean
1 cinnamon stick
1 large orange, blood orange if possible
1 cup dry sherry or red cooking wine
1 cup water
Sugar
1 tablespoon sunflower or canola oil

To prepare the quince: Steam quince for 10 minutes to make them easier to peel. Peel and quarter quince. Place quince into large heavy-bottom saucepan or copper jam-making pan. Open the vanilla bean and scrape seeds onto quince. Add cinnamon stick, orange zest and juice, sherry or wine, and water. Cook over high heat until fruit starts to get tender, in about 20 minutes. Let the fruit cool and then put it through a food mill to remove the pips and seeds.

Note: If you don't have a food mill, you can remove the core of the quinces before you cook them and then strain the fruit when it has finished cooking.

To make the paste: Weigh or measure the quince puree and put it back in the cooking pan. Measure an amount of sugar equal to the weight of the quince and add to the pan. Cook over medium-low heat, stirring often to avoid sticking on the bottom of the pan. Concentrate will turn from light pink to a rich orangey red shade—and begin to thicken—in 45–60 minutes. Quince paste is ready when it becomes a bit difficult to stir and a drop of it will "stand alone" and not flow as a liquid, similar to the process of jelly or jam making.

To set and store: Line a container (like a jelly roll pan) with wax paper or coat it with oil. Pour paste into container and let it set for 3 hours or overnight. Cut into cubes and put in airtight containers. It will keep for months in refrigerator.

To serve: Spread on toast for breakfast, offer with cheese as an appetizer, cut into small cubes and decorate meats for taste and aesthetics, or conclude dinner with a magnificent square of fruit with a cookie.

Brunch

Mac's Pumpkin Waffles

SERVES 4–6

When I lived on Capitol Hill in Washington, DC, I organized a playgroup, with another mother and a stay-at-home father named Mac Turner, for our year-old sons. These active little guys were a handful to manage as we each took turns one day a week for the next two years. Mac was a terrific "dad" to the boys. He built them a wooden slide down his cellar steps for indoor recreation in the winter and in other seasons pulled them along in a Red Flyer wood wagon to the local park or zoo. Mac's pumpkin waffles were a perfect finger food for these young guys. My son Nick and Mac are now adult friends and Nick still requests Mac's pumpkin waffles.

Equipment: Waffle maker

Dry ingredients:

2½ cups flour

2 tablespoons sugar

4 teaspoons baking powder

¼ teaspoon cream of tartar

½ teaspoon salt

1 teaspoon cinnamon

½ teaspoon ground ginger

¼ teaspoon ground nutmeg

⅛ teaspoon ground cloves

¾ cup chopped pecans or walnuts

Wet ingredients:

3 eggs

1½ cups milk

⅓ cup vegetable oil

1 cup pumpkin, pureed, or canned pumpkin pie filling

To prepare batter: Separate egg yolks, put in jar, refrigerate and save for another use since they will not be used in this recipe. Beat the egg whites with cream of tartar till they develop peaks. In one bowl, combine all dry ingredients except nuts. In another bowl, mix together all wet ingredients. Combine wet and dry ingredients, gently fold in egg whites, and add nuts.

To cook and serve: Cook in waffle iron and serve with butter, maple syrup, and fruit. As a dessert, serve with vanilla ice cream. Waffles freeze well and can be heated in a toaster.

Bread

Cheese Sticks with a Zing of Paprika

SERVES 20

Once you start eating these cheese sticks, it is hard to stop. Easy to make, they rival expensive store-bought cheese sticks. The secret ingredient is paprika, which adds a blush of color, helping them bake to a rich orange color, and adds that slight kick of flavor.

If you have a ravioli wheel, you can form decorative scalloped edges, but straight-edged bars of these goodies will disappear just as quickly. Serve them at your fanciest dinner party. I sometimes put a few in a cup at each place setting to be eaten with the soup course. My favorite, though, is to have them with Champagne as an appetizer. If you are not serving the cheese sticks for a party, you will want to cut this recipe in half (or make the whole quantity and freeze half.)

1½ pounds butter
6 cups flour
1 teaspoon paprika
1½ pounds sharp cheddar cheese, grated

To prepare dough: Mix all the ingredients in a large bowl. Knead till butter and cheese are well blended. Roll out on floured surface. Cut into 1 x 4-inch lengths. Place on cookie sheet.

To bake: Bake in a preheated oven at 375°F for 20 minutes.

Entrees

Veal Shanks with Parsnips, Carrots, Purple Kohlrabi, Potatoes, and Rosemary

SERVES 4

Your kitchen and the rest of the house will smell divine while this stew is cooking. The root vegetables add sweetness to the sauce and the meat will be falling off the bone when this dish is ready to devour.

Not only did I want to focus this cookbook on recipes that are easy for the home cook to prepare but I also wanted to offer recipes that can be made ahead of time. My personal preference is to have food with friends and not be in the kitchen.

If you can't find veal shanks, buy lamb shanks. They are economical and when cooked slowly with herbs, the meat will be infused with the flavor of the herbs.

½ cup all-purpose white flour

4 veal shanks

3 tablespoons olive oil

2 tablespoons butter

2 onions, sliced

2 cloves garlic, chopped fine

½ cup red wine

1½ quarts beef stock

4 parsnips cut in 3-inch lengths

4 carrots, cut into 4-inch lengths

2 medium kohlrabi, peeled and sliced in small wedges

6–8 baby potatoes with skins

1 (12-ounce) can of tomatoes, whole peeled

½ cup celery, chopped

1 tablespoon finely chopped fresh rosemary leaves

½ tablespoon finely chopped fresh thyme leaves

Salt and pepper to taste

For the garnish:

1 tablespoon coarsely chopped fresh parsley

To prepare veal shanks: Put flour on plate or in plastic bag and toss veal shanks in flour until coated. Put 2 tablespoons olive oil and butter in a heavy-bottom saucepan and, on high heat, brown shanks on all sides. Set aside. Scrape bottom of pan, add 1 tablespoon olive oil, and cook onions and garlic till light brown. Add the wine, stock, parsnips, carrots, kohlrabi, potatoes, tomatoes, celery, rosemary, thyme, and veal shanks. Bring to a boil, reduce heat, and simmer for 1 hour. Remove veal shanks and simmer liquid for 10–15 minutes until reduced to a sauce consistency.

To serve: Place shanks in large, shallow serving platter. Pour sauce over shanks and sprinkle with parsley for decoration.

Miss Patton's Shoulder Lamb Chops
with Mushrooms and Tomatoes

SERVES 4

My parents' good friend (Miss) Irene Patton, a terrific cook and English teacher, shared this recipe with my family. It was one of the first "grown-up" dishes I learned to cook. I had forgotten about the recipe until recently when I watched a *New York Times* video of Melissa Clark raving about the flavor and price of shoulder lamb chops. I was grateful to be able to find the recipe for this old favorite. I immediately sent it to my adult children, saying, "This is almost as easy as calling for carry-out. Try shoulder lamb chops. They are great and blend well with mushrooms in this recipe. You and your friends will love it." I hope you will too.

1 tablespoon butter

1 tablespoon olive oil

¼ cup onions, chopped

¼ cup cremini mushrooms, sliced

4 shoulder lamb chops

½ cup water

¼ teaspoon salt

¼ teaspoon celery salt

¾ teaspoon pepper

2 large tomatoes, cut in wedges

To prepare the lamb chops: Melt butter and olive oil in frying pan big enough to hold the chops. Sauté onion and mushrooms. Remove them from frying pan. Brown lamb chops on both sides for several minutes. Remove chops from pan. Deglaze pan with water and add spices. Place lamb chops back in pan, add the sautéed onions and mushrooms and cook covered for 30 minutes. Add tomato wedges and cook few more minutes till they are soft.

Torta Verde
(Green Tart)

SERVES 6–8

The name does not do justice to this "one-dish" meal. The delicate bottom and top crusts seal a moist interior. These tarts are called *torta* in Italian, and because its interior is mostly green, this one is called *torta verde*. There really isn't an American equivalent for this savory tart. The torta is made of flour, salt, and olive oil, more like a pizza crust. The simple crust contrasts well with the filling of greens, potato, egg, and cheese. Delicate swiss chard makes my favorite filling but collard or kale can be substituted. There are multiple greens being sold at regional wintertime farmers' markets in the heart of Massachusetts that you can use for this Italian "peasant" dish as a wonderful way to cook with healthy greens.

Equipment: Baking sheet

For the dough:

1¼ cups unbleached, unenriched white flour
½ teaspoon salt
1½ teaspoons olive oil
½ cup water

For the filling:

8–10 large leaves swiss chard, stems removed and leaves coarsely chopped
1½ tablespoons salt
1 large russet potato, washed and chopped
1 medium yellow onion, peeled and finely chopped
2 tablespoons minced fresh Italian parsley
1¼ cups crumbled feta cheese
Ground black pepper
2 eggs, lightly beaten
4 tablespoons olive oil

To make dough: Mix flour and salt in large bowl. Drizzle oil into flour. Add up to ½ cup water, mixing with large fork until the dough holds together. Knead dough for 10–15 minutes on floured board until the dough is smooth and elastic. Gather into ball, cover with damp dishtowel, and leave on counter or wrap in plastic and place in refrigerator. Let rest for 2 hours.

Prepare chard and potato: Put rinsed chard into colander, sprinkle salt on it, toss, and let drain for 20 minutes. Then press chard against sides of colander to squeeze out water. Boil potato in water until you can easily pierce a piece with a knife.

To prepare filling: Mix potato, onion, parsley, and feta, and season with salt and pepper. Add drained chard and eggs and 2½ tablespoons olive oil.

To make torta: Divide ball of dough into two pieces, one twice as big as the other. Roll out the larger piece (bottom of torta) on a floured surface into a circle approximately 14 inches in diameter. Gently fold in half by lifting one side over the other. Place on greased cookie sheet and unfold. Spread filling evenly over surface leaving a 1-inch border of dough around the edges. Roll out the smaller piece of dough to make the top for the torta, about 13 inches in diameter. Place this piece of dough on top of filling. Using a pastry brush, wet bottom edge of dough with water. Then turn bottom edge of dough up over the top piece of dough. Press down on edges to create a seal, making some small indentations every few inches (not continuously like a pie). Poke some holes in top of dough to allow steam to escape. Drizzle top with remaining 1½ tablespoons olive oil.

To bake: Preheat oven to 375° and bake 35 minutes until top is golden. Cool on rack. Serve warm and cut into pie slices. There you have it: carbohydrates, protein, and vegetables all in one slice.

Meatballs with Coco Tomato Sauce

SERVES 5–6

I always distrusted meatballs. What type of meat were they made of? Would they sit heavily in my stomach and weigh me down all day? We didn't even have spaghetti and meatballs as a comfort food at home. Therefore I was skeptical when I ordered meatballs with tomato sauce served on polenta at Coco and The Cellar Bar in Easthampton. Wow, what a game changer. Delicious, light, slightly crunchy exterior and delicious interior, these meatballs were served in a delectable tomato sauce contrasting with the texture of the corn polenta. Yum. You will file away this recipe for special occasions.

Equipment: Deep-fry thermometer (optional)

For the sauce:

2 tablespoons olive oil
½ cup finely chopped yellow onion
1 small carrot, finely chopped
1 stalk celery, finely chopped
2 cloves garlic, minced
1 teaspoon finely chopped thyme
1 (28-ounce) can whole peeled tomatoes
1 cup chicken stock
1 tablespoon salt, or to taste

For the meatballs:

1 pound ground turkey (thighs, if available)
1 pound ground pork
2 teaspoons salt, or to taste
¼ cup olive oil
1 small yellow onion, finely chopped
2 cloves garlic, minced
¼ cup finely chopped Italian parsley
1 tablespoon finely chopped thyme
½ teaspoon red chile flakes (optional)
2 cups panko or homemade bread crumbs
¼ cup grated Parmesan cheese, plus more for serving
2 eggs, lightly beaten
Vegetable oil, for frying

To prepare sauce: Heat 2 tablespoons olive oil in saucepan over medium heat. Add onion, carrot, and celery and sauté over medium heat until translucent and soft. Don't allow vegetables to brown. Stir in garlic, thyme, tomatoes, and chicken stock and bring to a simmer. Reduce heat to low and simmer sauce for 30 minutes. Season with salt and transfer to food processor, pulsing briefly just to break up tomatoes.

To make meatballs: Place turkey and pork in a medium-size bowl and add 1 teaspoon salt. Mix just enough to combine ingredients. Set aside. Heat olive oil, reserving 2 tablespoons, over medium heat in medium-size saucepan. Add onion and cook until soft and translucent. Turn off heat and stir in garlic, parsley, thyme, and chile flakes, if using. Combine onion mixture with panko or bread crumbs, Parmesan cheese, remaining 2 tablespoons olive oil, and salt to taste in a large bowl. Gently mix in the ground meat, then eggs, being very careful not to overmix. With damp hands, form into 15 meatballs.

To cook meatballs: In a large, straight-sided skillet over medium heat, add enough oil to reach halfway up the sides of the pan. When a deep-fry thermometer reaches 350°F, fry meatballs in batches, being sure not to overcrowd. Turn meatballs frequently until they are uniformly golden brown and transfer to a 13 x 9-inch baking pan.

To assemble: Cover meatballs with tomato sauce, then bake in preheated 350°F oven until sauce in the middle of the dish is bubbling, about 20–30 minutes.

To serve: Serve on polenta and top with grated cheese.

Soups

Chestnut Soup

SERVES 4

Chestnuts were an important part of the diet of Native Americans living in Massachusetts, west of the Connecticut River in areas now called the Berkshires and Pioneer Valley. Like most nuts, chestnuts have rich properties like folic acid, vitamin C, dietary fiber, and contain no gluten. No wonder the colonists adopted chestnuts and included them in various dishes, especially soups and stuffing. The magnificent New England chestnut trees, their nuts with spiky outer husks and glistening inner seeds, were mostly wiped out by blight, but there are many ongoing efforts to revive the trees. In any case, chestnuts are always available in the market, especially for Thanksgiving and Christmas cooking, and cooking with them is a reminder of Berkshire and Pioneer Valley traditions.

For the soup:

3 cups prepared whole roasted chestnuts or 5 cups shelled chestnuts

2 cups coarsely chopped onion

¾ cup thinly sliced carrots

1 tablespoon olive oil

3 cups chicken stock or canned broth

Salt and pepper, to taste

2 tablespoons butter

2 tablespoons dry sherry

1 cup heavy whipping cream (optional)

1 bouquet garni (1 sprig each of thyme and parsley, and a bay leaf)

For the garnish:

Greek-style yogurt

Few pieces of candied ginger, finely sliced

To prepare chestnuts: Cut X on flat portion of each chestnut. Roast in 400°F oven until pieces of shell around the X peel back. Cool chestnuts and take off shell and skin close to chestnut. Return to baking pan and bake for 20 minutes till roasted. Chop into coarse pieces. If you use shelled chestnuts from a jar or vacuum-sealed package, remove from package and coarsely chop.

To prepare soup: Put onions and carrots in small bowl and toss with olive oil. Place on baking pan and bake for 1 hour at 400°F, flipping occasionally, till vegetables are tender.

Next step: Puree vegetables and chestnuts in batches in food processor and place in saucepan. Add stock, salt and pepper to taste, butter, sherry, and cream, plus bouquet garni. Bring to a simmer at medium-high heat. Reduce heat and simmer 20 minutes. Whisk frequently to prevent scorching.

To serve: Garnish with dollop of Greek-style yogurt and tiny pieces of candied ginger.

Farro Soup with Winter Root Vegetables

SERVES 4

Farro is also known as spelt, emmer, and einkorn. These ancient grains fascinated me while I was writing my bread baking book. The nutritional value of these grains is outstanding since they haven't been overbred by the big agribusiness companies in their quest to have the world plant their uniform bland grains. In spite of all my work with ancient grains, I wasn't as familiar with using them in salads and soups. Then just one farro soup, and I fell in love with their taste and chewy texture.

To me, soups I love fall into two categories. One is potages, creamy soups I learned to love in France, and the second type is a soup with "stuff in it to hunt for." After all, I grew up in the alphabet soup and popular minestrone era, when looking for ingredients was a ploy to keep children interested in eating a soup. Today there are recipes for more imaginative soups such as this one, with its root vegetables spiked with the flavor of deep red *guajillo* chiles which, Wikipedia tells me, "contain a green tea flavor with berry overtones." Green tea of the East meets chile of of the South meets traditional root vegetables of the West.

For the soup:

4 baby turnips
1 (1 pound or less) small squash, kabocha, butternut, or other type
4–5 carrots
4 parsnips
3 stalks celery
5 small potatoes
3 onions
5–7 stalks kale
1 dried guajillo or ancho chile
3 tablespoons olive oil
2 garlic cloves, minced
1 bay leaf
5 sprigs fresh thyme, leaves pulled from stem, finely chopped
½ teaspoon salt, or to taste
Vegetable broth

For the farro:

2 cups farro

For the garnish:

Parmesan or Parmigiano-Reggiano cheese
2 tablespoons finely chopped parsley

To prepare vegetables: Peel turnips and squash. Dice into 1- to 2-inch cubes. Cut carrots, parsnips, and celery into ½-inch pieces. Leave skins on potatoes and cut them into 1- to 2-inch cubes. Peel and coarsely chop onions. Remove any large stems from the kale (especially at bottom) and pull into medium-size pieces. Pull stem off chile and shake out seeds if desired (though this chile is mild and I cook it with the seeds.)

To sauté: In a large saucepan, sauté onion for 2 minutes in olive oil, then add garlic and sauté 1 minute longer. Add the turnips, squash, carrots, parsnips, celery, potatoes, bay leaf, thyme, salt, and chile and just enough broth to cover. Cook 20 minutes until vegetables are soft but not mushy. Add the kale and cook until kale is slightly wilted. Remove chile before serving vegetables and broth.

In the meantime: According to directions on package, cook farro in water or vegetable broth for about 25 minutes until it is tender but still has some "bite" or chewiness. Drain.

To serve: Put ½ cup farro in each bowl. Spoon vegetables and some broth into bowl. Grate some Parmigiano-Reggiano cheese over top. Sprinkle with parsley.

Salads

Marinated Celery Root Salad

SERVES 4

Celery root is an undervalued vegetable and I hope you will try it immediately. It's an ugly duck-ling—a knobby, round root of brown and white. Many European cooks serve it regularly; the French often offer it as an appetizer plate. Now you'll find it in almost every American farmers' mar-ket. I hope you will enjoy its woodsy taste and terrific crunch. Marinated celery root (often called celery root remoulade on menus) is a good partner with grilled salmon.

2 pounds celery root
1¾ teaspoons salt
3 tablespoons lemon juice
1 cup good quality mayonnaise
¼ cup Dijon mustard
2 tablespoons horseradish, fresh grated or from jar
2 teaspoons white wine vinegar
Freshly ground black pepper

To prepare the celery root: Cut off the outer skin of the celery root with a sharp knife and remove hard bottom. Ideally, you should cut the root into fine, julienned match-sticks about 3 inches long, but you can also grate the celery root on a grater.

To prepare the sauce: Combine salt, lemon juice, may-onnaise, mustard, horseradish, and wine vinegar in bowl. Marinate the celery root in the sauce for several hours.

To serve: Place lettuce leaves, like Boston lettuce, on salad plates. Serve celery root on top and grind some fresh pepper on each serving.

Grated Beet Salad with Anise in Yogurt Dressing

SERVES 4

Already a (boiled) beet lover, I've enjoyed exploring the world of roasted and raw beets. Farmers are selling beets in glorious colors—yellow, orange, variegated. This salad introduces the Mediterranean flavors of orange, lemon, and olive oil. The star anise takes us to the Orient. The salad can be laid on top of couscous for a luncheon plate or used as a salad with a dinner meal.

½ pound beets

3 tablespoons freshly squeezed orange juice

1 tablespoon freshly squeezed lemon juice

1 tablespoon extra-virgin olive oil

2 tablespoons finely minced chives, mint, or parsley (or a combination)

½ teaspoon salt

2 star anise pods, crushed in mortar and pestle, or 1 teaspoon ground anise

1 pound arugula

To prepare: Peel the skin off beets with a vegetable peeler. Grate the beets with a hand grater (large opening) or food processor fitted with the shredding blade. Combine the orange juice, lemon juice, olive oil, herbs (chives, mint, or parsley), plus salt and star anise. Toss the herbs with the marinade and beets. Let marinate for a couple of hours. Toss with yogurt dressing. (Dressing will turn pink.)

To serve: Place arugula on a serving platter and arrange beets on top.

Note: It is possible to store the marinated beets in tight-lidded container for several days. The beets will become tender but will not lose their texture.

Yogurt Dressing

MAKES SEVERAL SERVINGS

I always feel good when I use this dressing. It tastes wholesome and there is a happy yin-yang between the sweet syrup and bitter vinegar.

1 cup plain yogurt

3 tablespoons maple syrup

1 teaspoon wine vinegar

1 teaspoon paprika

1 teaspoon salt

To prepare: Combine all ingredients. Blend with small whisk or fork or place in small bottle and shake. Refrigerate any leftover dressing.

Desserts

Chocolate Cherry Pudding Cake

SERVES 12

This cake recipe is a revival of a popular 19th-century cake called "pudding cake," which consists of a cake batter placed in a pan with hot water poured over it. The whole thing sounded awful when a friend offered to bring it to party. I wanted to say, "Don't bother." I envisioned a soggy-bottomed cake, but—surprise—the cake is divine and now I make it myself just to elicit raves. The final outcome is a cake with the normal consistency of cake on top, yet soft and warm on the bottom, a bit like a soufflé. Put it in the oven while your guests are enjoying their main course. The cake must be served warm since it is that soft, warm texture that is reminiscent of a soufflé. You will be able to serve "soufflé" without the anxiety of whether it has properly risen or not. If you wish, offer guests ice cream or whipped cream with the cake, truly a wonderful, delicious treat.

For the cake batter:

8 tablespoons butter

4 ounces chocolate, dark unsweetened

1½ cups milk

2 eggs

4 teaspoons vanilla

2½ cups flour

1 cup sugar

4 teaspoons baking powder

½ cup walnuts

15 cherries, pitted

For the topping:

6 tablespoons cocoa, good quality

1 cup sugar

2 cups water, boiling

To prepare cake: Melt butter and chocolate in medium-size saucepan. Stir in milk, eggs, and vanilla. Combine flour, sugar, and baking powder in a bowl. Gradually add dry ingredients to wet ingredients, mixing lightly. Scatter walnuts and 10–15 cherries on bottom of a greased 9 x 13-inch glass pan and pour cake batter into pan.

To prepare topping: Mix cocoa with sugar. Sprinkle over cake batter. Boil water and pour over the entire cake batter.

To bake: Transfer pan to preheated oven at 350°F. Cake is done when it springs back to touch and liquid-pudding is bubbling.

Holiday Dutch Stollen

SERVES 8

Is this Dutch stollen a Berkshire food? Yes, stollen has made its way to the Berkshires via many sources, including French-Canadian master baker Richard Bourdon. When Richard lived and baked in the Netherlands, he learned to make a marvelous stollen (different from German-style stollen). Imagine my surprise when I worked at the Berkshire Mountain Bakery and saw Richard making the same style of Dutch stollen that my Dutch mother made every Christmas, with a roll of almond paste at its center. Richard's recipe was for hundreds of stollen, and my mother's was for twenty. But, just for you, I have adjusted their recipes for a single stollen. I didn't want you to buy any of the vulgar stollen sold in stores. Homemade stollen is so much better. Having taught this recipe in cooking classes, I know it is easy, makes a great gift, and keeps well.

For the stollen:

2½ cups unbleached white flour
2 teaspoons baking powder
¾ cup sugar
½ teaspoon salt
¼ teaspoon mace
⅛ teaspoon cardamom
¾ cup ground blanched almonds
¼ cup butter
1 cup ricotta cheese
1 egg
½ teaspoon vanilla
¼ teaspoon almond extract
2 tablespoons rum
½ cup golden raisins
½ cup currants
¼ cup candied lemon peel, chopped
(Or substitute candied orange peel or candied ginger, but don't buy the dyed candied fruits used in fruit cakes.)

For the almond paste interior:

1 cup almond paste (not marzipan)
1 egg yolk
¼ cup sugar

For the topping:

3 tablespoons butter, melted
3 tablespoons vanilla sugar (sugar infused with vanilla bean)

To prepare ahead:

Vanilla sugar: Bury a split vanilla bean in 1 cup of sugar inside a jar with a closed lid for several days or weeks. (There are years when I remember to do this ahead and other years when I don't. Just use plain sugar if you forget.)

Ground almonds: Pulverize blanched almonds in a food processor. It's also possible to buy ground almonds.

Raisins and currants: Soak raisins and currants in rum until ready to use.

Almond paste: Mix the almond paste, egg yolk, and sugar and roll into sausage about 8 inches long. Chill.

To make the stollen:

Dry mixture: Combine flour, baking powder, sugar, salt, mace, cardamom, and ground almonds. Cut butter into mixture either using two knives with a criss-crossing action or working quickly with your fingers to break up butter into flour until the texture is the consistency of coarse crumbs.

Wet mixture: Place cheese, egg, vanilla, almond extract, raisins and currants soaked in rum, and lemon peel into bowl. Mix the wet and dry mixture together and stir until the mixture is moist. Generously flour the surface where you will place the dough (especially if the dough is somewhat wet). Roll out into an oval shape 8 x 10 inches. Melt 1 tablespoon butter and, with pastry brush, spread melted butter on top of dough. Make a crease in the center with the rolling pin. Place almond paste in this indentation. Then fold over to enclose the almond paste in the center.

To bake: Place on parchment paper or a flattened piece of brown paper shopping bag. (I don't know if my mother didn't have parchment paper handy, but she always baked her stollen on unfolded brown paper bags.) Bake at 350°F for 45 minutes or longer. Bake till surface is light brown.

To decorate: Place clean towel under a cooling rack to catch sugar. Take stollen out of the oven and place on rack. Using pastry brush, cover surface with melted butter and pour vanilla sugar over stollen. Let cool. Later, turn stollen over and tap off excess sugar. (Don't be afraid of the butter—it makes the stollen moist and helps it keep longer.)

To keep: Wrap stollen in aluminum foil. The flavor mellows as it ages. Wrap with a ribbon and decorate with a holly leaf (hand cut from square of green felt) and a red berry.

Restaurants

Blantyre

Executive Chef: Arnaud Cotar
Lenox

Blantyre has had a fascinating history. Built by a wealthy Scottish-American owner to be one of the grandest Gilded Age country houses in the Berkshires, Blantyre was designed to resemble the Scottish ancestral home of the owner's mother. Blantyre exemplifies a Tudor-style castle with architectural features such as towers, turrets, gargoyles, and leaded windows. When construction began in 1901, over three hundred people were employed building the castle and outbuildings and designing and planting the grounds. Furniture and decorative objects were brought from England and Scotland and the house served as a lavish entertaining site in the summer season.

Photo © Blantyre

Photo © Sean McLaughlin

But the Gilded Age's extravagant lifestyle and unprecedented economic growth began to decline around the turn of the century. After World War I, and for the next sixty years, Blantyre went through many transitions until it was bought for less than $300,000 in a bankruptcy sale in the 1980s by John and Jane Fitzpatrick, the owners of the Red Lion Inn and one of the country's early mail-order businesses, Country Curtains. By then the Fitzpatricks had learned a lot about restoring large properties, thanks to their restoration efforts on The Red Lion Inn, one of the oldest inns in continuous use in New England, a facility that also served as the headquarters for the Country Curtain business. John and Jane Fitzpatrick bought Blantyre for their daughter Ann, as they had already given daughter Nancy the Red Lion Inn. Ann and her mother Jane spent years and significant sums restoring Blantyre before opening it as a boutique hotel in 1981.

Today, Blantyre describes itself as an elegant home, "a place reminiscent of gentler times of romance and elegance." Indeed, Blantyre is a five-star exclusive luxury country-house hotel and member of Relais & Châteaux, a group of hotels and restaurants that meet the extremely high standards of that organization. Owner Ann Fitzpatrick Brown was raised by parents deeply immersed in restoring a traditional inn, and she demonstrates all she has learned as she manages the decor, dining, service, and other offerings of Blantyre. The owner comments that the popularity

Photo © George Ross

of *Downton Abbey* causes guests to compare staying at Blantyre to having their own Downton Abbey in the form of a Scottish castle, fully staffed with housekeepers, flower arrangers, a sommelier, and chefs to meet their every need and desire.

Blantyre is a magnificent place with large fireplaces in the main rooms on the first floor, hand-carved woodwork and mantels, an octagonal breakfast room, glass-enclosed conservatory, wood-paneled dining room, overstuffed furniture, and elegant furnishings and antiques. It's a small hotel and a truly private sanctuary. Blantyre has twenty-one rooms—ten suites and eight rooms in the main house and four cottages on the property—and therefore every guest has the full attention of the Blantyre staff. In the summer, activities listed on Blantyre's website include "lounging" and "hammock." What a lovely way to describe what is at the heart of the Blantyre experience—an atmosphere of encouraging guests to relax. For more vigorous activities, tennis and swimming in a heated pool are popular. Recently Blantyre added a full spa facility, a feature that appeals to a younger guest set. The spa offers a full range of body and beauty treatments.

In 2005 Blantyre was opened, for the first time, during the winter season. Winterizing the house was a big undertaking for the large estate. Each Thanksgiving the 105-foot tree at the top of the road leading to the estate is lit to inaugurate the new winter holiday season at Blantyre. A winter concierge helps guests plan winter activities, such as snowshoeing, cross-country skiing on trails through the 117-acre property, riding in a horse-drawn sleigh, and even ice-skating on the tennis court. As soon as the weather is cold enough, the tennis court is magically transformed into a skating rink, with lights draped from the high fences of the court, tables and chairs placed on the ice where guests can take a brief rest (with legs warmed by lap blankets) or sip hot chocolate with real marshmallows. Adjoining the tennis court is a sweet cottage, the Warming Hut, with red Chinese furniture, huge fireplace, and pool table—a place to get warm before another round of skating. What could be more fantastic than oysters on snowballs or a Cointreau hot chocolate? Blantyre offers a Snow Barbeque served at the rink with a menu ranging from marinated prime New York strip steak to fig-and-orange bread pudding. The staff works hard to give their guests a taste of an aristocratic, pampered lifestyle with impeccable service.

Dining is a whole event unto itself. The wood-paneled dining room undergoes a transformation just before "cocktail hour." Tables are set with jacquard linens, William Yeoward crystal, fine china like Limoges, and sterling silver place settings. A piano or harp quietly plays in the background. If guests wish, sometimes a private table can be set in the library, just for them.

French Chef Arnaud Cotar and his wife, Christelle, wine director, are the husband-and-wife team who make the dining experience at Blantyre a one-of-a-kind experience, with the help of sommelier Luc Chevalier. Chef Cotar lived above his family's restaurant as a child, working as a

waiter and helper in the kitchen. Later, he attended culinary school in France and worked at top restaurants in England, before coming to Blantyre as the sous chef, and where he is now chef. His French-born wife also trained in France and assists the sommelier with the wine cellar of seventeen thousand bottles. Dining is prix-fixe between $125 and $165. One thoughtful alteration to summertime dinner service is the option of late dessert on the nights when the Boston Symphony Orchestra is playing at Tanglewood. After the concert, a buffet of dessert and cheese is ready for the concertgoing guests to enjoy as they relax and reflect on the concert. This nod to the Boston Symphony Orchestra might be due to Ann's mother's long service as a board member and philanthropist to the Symphony.

Forbes has awarded Blantyre five stars since 2003 for its hospitality and dining experiences. Being at Blantyre is like stepping into another era. Its privacy, exclusivity, and elegance are a rare treat for those who come to stay here.

French Beef Stew with Vegetables

SERVES 8

Chef Arnout Cotar reflects his French heritage and culinary training in this rich beef stew for the elite clients at Blantyre, an elegant boutique hotel in the Berkshires. You can replicate this dish thanks to the generosity of Blantyre and Chef Cotar sharing the recipe for this book.

Equipment: Heavy braising pot (dutch oven–style) with cover

For the stew:

3 tablespoons olive oil
4 pounds beef chuck cut into 1½-inch chunks, lightly salted and peppered
1 medium onion
1 carrot
1 leek
3 celery stalks
6 cloves garlic, peeled
4 sprigs thyme
6 stems parsley
1 teaspoon peppercorns
1 bottle dry red wine, like Cabernet
2½ quarts veal (or beef) stock

For the garnish:

25–30 pearl onions
Pinch salt and pepper
2 large carrots
1 tablespoon butter
Small handful finely minced parsley
2 cups of your favorite mushrooms

Step One

To prepare: In hot oil, brown the seasoned meat on all sides and transfer to a large bowl. Roughly chop the vegetables and add to the bowl along with the herbs. Pour in enough wine to cover all the ingredients and marinate in the refrigerator for 2 days.

Step Two

To prepare: Put meat and vegetable mixture into a heavy braising pot with a cover (a dutch oven like the Le Creuset brand heavy stockpot is ideal). Add the veal (or beef) stock. Bring to a simmer and be sure the liquid does not boil. Cover and slowly cook until meat is tender (but not falling apart), about 3 hours. Cool completely in the cooking liquid. Scoop out all the cooled meat chunks and set aside. Bring the liquid that remains in the braising pot to a slow boil, then lower to simmer and cook uncovered until a rich, winey flavor develops and the consistency is dense and dark. Depending on the volume of liquid in the pot, it could take 45 minutes to a little over an hour. While it's still hot, strain and pour hot liquid mixture over the reserved meat. Adjust the seasonings. The meat and sauce are ready but the flavor will be enhanced if the dish is refrigerated for a day or two.

To prepare garnish: Peel pearl onions and lightly coat with oil, season with salt and pepper, and roast in preheated oven at 325°F until golden brown and tender. Peel and cut the carrots into 2- to 3-inch lengths and place in single layer in a large pan. Barely cover with water and add 2 tablespoons of butter. Cover and cook until fork tender. Uncover and keep cooking until the buttery liquid glazes the carrots. Toss carrots with the chopped parsley. For the mushrooms, slice and sauté in butter with pinch of salt and pepper until tender.

To serve: Place beef stew and sauce in large serving dish. Decoratively arrange the onions, carrots, and mushrooms.

Photo © Blantyre

The Red Lion Inn

Executive Chef: Brian Alberg
Stockbridge

Inns are usually just inns. Places to spend the night and get some food. But The Red Lion Inn distinguishes itself as an inn involved in a pivotal eighteenth-century event in our nation's history and, especially in recent years due to the philanthropic and public service role of its owners, as a leading institution in making a positive impact on the local Berkshire community.

The Red Lion Inn in Stockbridge is a large white clapboard inn with a wide veranda located directly on Main Street. Made famous by Norman Rockwell's painting, *Main Street at Christmas,* The Red Lion Inn has 125 guest rooms, some in the main structure and others in adjoining properties. There are several dining options in the Inn—from casual to traditional, indoors and out. The heated swimming pool is an added feature. The Red Lion Inn is one of the few New England inns operating continuously since the eighteenth century.

In 1773, a general store on the site of today's Red Lion Inn, evolved into a stagecoach stop and then a full-fledged tavern and inn. The owners, Silas and Anna Bingham, called their inn, The Red Lion Inn with the lion being the symbol of the British government. Supposedly, the green tail of the Lion was meant as a quiet message of sympathy to the independent spirit stirring in the region.

Photo by Lauren Delorenzo/Courtesy of The Red Lion Inn

Photo by Lauren Delorenzo/Courtesy of The Red Lion Inn

When Silas died in 1781, Anna took over the Inn and became the first businesswoman in the Berkshires. A few years later, in 1786, the Inn was reported to have been "invaded and taken over for a while by the Shay's Rebellion forces." Shay's Rebellion might not be remembered by every American history student, but the local uprising caused the federal government to consider the extent of its powers in the writing of the Constitution and was one of the reasons Washington was recruited to run for president and bring stability to the country.

Charles and Mert Plumb purchased the Inn in 1862, expanding it. Mert Plumb might be considered one of the region's first interior decorators, as she undertook the trendsetting task of purchasing and appropriately placing antique furniture and china in the Inn. Teapots, which sit on shelves in the Inn today, were purchased by Mrs. Plumb. By the mid-1800s, Stockbridge was transformed into a literary and artistic community. Railroad lines to Stockbridge made it easier to reach the Berkshires, and the region was discovered by wealthy families who began to build grand estates. By the middle of the century, money was flowing, and some truly magnificent homes were erected in and around Stockbridge. These sophisticated travelers were attracted to The Red Lion Inn with its fine menu and tasteful furnishings.

A fire nearly destroyed the Inn in 1895, but the owners were able to reopen the Inn two years later, with many of the original furnishings collected by Mrs. Plumb saved from destruction. In 1955 the 90-year dynasty of the family owners ended, and the Inn began to struggle. By 1968 the Inn was in financial trouble, and the owners were contemplating selling the property to replace it with a garage and gas station.

When John "Jack" Fitzpatrick bought the Inn, he intended to use it as the location for the ever-expanding mail order business, Country Curtains, which he and his wife Jane had launched. But Jane and Jack fell in love with the historic building and soon began a major restoration with a new kitchen and revamped dining spaces. Eventually, they purchased some neighboring buildings such as the Village Firehouse and period houses and converted them for additional guest rooms. Jack served four terms in the Massachusetts legislature and was deeply involved as a civic leader in Stockbridge. He and Jane together or separately, served on many cultural and community boards. As their Country Curtains business expanded and succeeded, the Fitzpatricks established a family foundation, High Meadows Foundation, and made philanthropic leadership investments in local schools and various performing arts and cultural institutions in the Berkshires. Jane Fitzpatrick, for example, helped save the struggling Berkshire Theatre Festival, served on the boards of the Boston Symphony Orchestra, Norman Rockwell Museum, and MASS MoCA.

Having enjoyed bringing the Inn to life and being involved in all aspects of its operations and the community, the Fitzpatricks bought another neglected property in nearby Lenox, called Blantyre in 1980. Their daughter, Ann Fitzpatrick Brown, owns and operates Blantyre, while they gave The Red Lion Inn to their daughter Nancy. Following the deaths of Jack and Jane Fitzpatrick, the baton for The Red Lion Inn has been passed to their daughter Nancy, who is the owner and president, and her stepdaughter Sarah Eustis, the managing director. These two women are leaders in a new company founded in 2013, Main Street Hospitality Group which now manages The Red Lion Inn, Williams Inn in Williamstown, The Porches in at MASS MoCA in North Adams, and Hotel on North, a Pittsfield hotel opened in 2015. Inspired by their muse Jane, the family is carrying on her emphasis to administer the properties with "sustainability, eco-conscious practices and support for the community."

The Red Lion Inn participates in using BerkShares, a form of currency printed and exchanged in the Berkshires. It is not monopoly money. It is real and incorporates the same security features as US currency. In fact, it is handsome currency printed with regional scenes and significant local leaders. The Inn and people in the Berkshires are serious about supporting their local economy, especially its food and cultural scene.

The choice of Chef Brian Alberg is in keeping with The Red Lion Inn's sustainability mission. Brian is executive chef of the Inn as well as holding the position of Vice President of Food & Beverage for Main Street Hospitality Group. Like many celebrity chefs, Brian is loyal to his "home" kitchen, producing six hundred dinners on Christmas day at the Inn, as well as overseeing the food and wine at other properties. The day I tried to catch up with him for a food photo shoot, he was rushing back from advising at the Williams Inn, one of Main Street's new acquisitions.

Brian is a leader in the local Berkshire food movement, including being the founding chair of Berkshire Farm & Table, an organization growing the Berkshires economically by advancing the food scene, promoting the region as a food tourism destination. I first met Brian at special events in the region, such as in 2012 at the Outstanding in the Field Berkshires event, where he was the selected guest chef. The event was held at the beautiful Indian Line Farm, the first CSA in North America. As a mentor to at-risk youth in the Railroad Street Youth Project in Great Barrington, Brian helps teens receive culinary arts training and skills. Besides admiring Brian for his commitment to Berkshire and Hudson Valley food producers, I appreciate his openness and willingness to promote other chefs, especially up-and-coming chefs in the region. The Inn benefits from Brian's adherence to tradition with an inventive twist, its ecological mission and support of BerkShares currency. The Red Lion Inn is steeped in history yet operates as an entrepreneurial business. Visit and enjoy the Inn at any season of the year.

Poached Hakurei Turnips with Caramelized Bacon and Smoky Tomato Sauce

SERVES 4

Bacon and charred tomatoes bring smoky sweetness to turnips cooked in goose fat. This recipe comes from Executive Chef Brian Alberg of The Red Lion Inn in Stockbridge, Massachusetts.

½ cup packed light brown sugar

8 slices thick-cut bacon

3 pounds plum tomatoes, cored

2 tablespoons olive oil

2⅓ cups chicken stock

4 cloves garlic, thinly sliced

3 large shallots, thinly sliced

1 cup packed basil leaves

1 tablespoon Worcestershire sauce

Kosher salt and ground black pepper, to taste

1 cup rendered goose fat (olive oil can be used as a substitute)

2 pounds Hakurei turnips, peeled and cut into 1½-inch chunks

4 cloves garlic, crushed

4 sprigs thyme

To prepare bacon and tomatoes: Sprinkle sugar over bacon on a baking sheet and bake in 425°F oven till crisp and glazed, about 16 minutes. Cool, cut into 1-inch pieces, and set aside. Heat oven to broil. Broil tomatoes on a foil-lined baking sheet until charred all over, about 20 minutes. Heat oil in a 10-inch skillet over medium-high heat. Add tomatoes, ⅓ cup stock, garlic, and shallots; cook until tomatoes break down, about 10 minutes. Puree with basil, Worcestershire, and salt and pepper; set aside.

To prepare turnips: Heat fat in a 12-inch skillet over medium-high heat. Add turnips; cook until starting to soften, about 20 minutes. Add tomato stock, garlic, thyme, salt and pepper; boil. Reduce heat to medium-low; cook, covered, until tender, about 20 minutes. Serve turnips atop tomato sauce and garnish with bacon.

Photo left, by Lauren Delorenzo; right, Kris Krough; both courtesy of The Red Lion Inn

Food Producers

Mayval Farm

Parsons Family
Westhampton

Maple Syrup. It's gold in color and, like the metal, a precious commodity. It takes approximately forty gallons of sap to produce just one gallon of maple syrup and it takes a lot of effort to produce that one gallon. In addition, there is also the tricky factor of weather: One year the right weather conditions will let the sap flow for as many as eight weeks, but a burst of warm weather can shorten the season to a month.

If you'd like to see maple syrup being made, come by Mayval Farm toward the end of February or early March. The Parsons family still lives on the 350-acre Mayval Farm, which was founded by Noah Parson III in 1778 in Westhampton. Now many generations later, two brothers, Ed and Henry, their wives Margie and Tina, and four children pitch in as a team to make a couple hundred gallons of maple syrup. First, they drill holes in the trunks of the sugar maples. When I interviewed Margie Parsons, she mentioned that this step needs to be performed "thoughtfully." It's important to "respect" the tree and only bore the right number of holes on a tree, based on its diameter and age. The boring must be done gently to avoid damaging the trees, and the hole must be cleaned of wood chips with a brush or twigs (no leaning over and blowing air into the hole; it might cause contamination).

The next step is to hang approximately 1,200 metal buckets on the trees. As the sap rises, some of it drips into the buckets, where it stays cool and fresh. Many sugarbush farms, as maple syrup–producing farms are called, use plastic tubing to carry the sap directly to the sugar house, where the sap is boiled. But there are still questions in the industry about how to clean the tubing and keep a consistent flow of sap to avoid the dangers of bacteria and yeast. The Parsons stick to old-fashioned methods. But using individual buckets means that humans must gather the sap—several times—from each of the 1,200 buckets! Each individual bucket is taken off the tree by family and friends and emptied into a three-hundred-gallon tank, which is then hauled to the sugaring house with a tractor and emptied into a huge thousand-gallon storage tank.

The most critical step in making maple syrup is the "evaporation" stage. When the sap is lowered from the thousand-gallon tank into an evaporator (which does exactly what its name says, evaporates), the clear sap is boiled until it is reduced into a thicker golden syrup. The Parsons family still boil their syrup over a traditional wood-burning fire. It is a very primal activity to cook the clear sap and transform it into a sweet, golden syrup. Ed Parsons continually monitors the color and thickness of the syrup with a hydrometer. The first few boilings produce light syrup, called "fancy" syrup. It takes a master syrup maker to produce really fine light syrup and Ed, like his father before him, is highly skilled in making this delicacy. Mayval Farm's fancy syrup is so fine that other sugar bush farms even buy it to sell to their customers because they can't produce enough of their own.

One of the final phases is to filter out the "sugar sand," small crystals of sugar. These crystals have no ill effects, but they make for spots of gritty texture instead of consistently smooth syrup. Maple syrup must be packaged while it is hot and then cooled. Maple syrup used to be graded and awarded letters (AA-B) with no national uniform regulations. Recently, the industry has decided to use universal categories: *Golden* in color with delicate flavor, *Amber* with rich flavor, *Dark* with robust flavor and *Very Dark* with strong flavor.

The Parsons save a bit of their syrup to use for making maple-sugar candy. Making candy involves heating the syrup to a soft-ball stage and then pouring it into molds (usually in the form of maple leaves), where it crystalizes and turns into candy. Another special product is maple cream. To make that, maple syrup is heated to 235°F on a candy thermometer, then cooled off to 100°F in an ice bath before it is beaten until it becomes thick and creamy and a soft beige color. Packaged in small containers, maple cream may not be gold in color, but good maple cream is highly prized.

There is always a maple-syrup product that is spontaneously made right at the sugar house, usually by the children. I remember making maple-sugar snow candy when I went to visit a cousin in New Hampshire. We'd walk to a local sugaring house and ask for a cup of maple sugar, then pour it on the snow where it would become the consistency of taffy. It was delicious, and my mother would pack some away in our lunches when we went skiing, if we had managed to bring some home to be stored and didn't eat it all on the spot.

For many years, the Parsons sold maple-syrup products in a front room hall of the house. Customers would knock, come in, and be served or help themselves. The Parsons will continue to make maple syrup on the farm, but they are now adding a farm store and making cheese.

Thanks to a Massachusetts Department of Agriculture Viability Grant, the Parsons embarked on a new project—making their own cheeses from the milk of their hundred dairy cows and selling farm products at a farm store. The process of planning and securing permits took two years. Finally the Parsons held a soft opening in February 2015 and are looking forward to selling some of the farm products at a small farm store this summer, and taking their cheeses, fresh milk (with chilled little eight-ounce bottles of plain and chocolate milk for kids), and maple products to the local farmers' markets this summer. The Parsons are also considering collaborating with some CSAs that are interested in carrying their products.

One of only 150 dairy farms left in the state, Mayval Farm has been a producer of excellent milk that is sold and used in many well-known brands such as Cabot cheese and Hood dairy products. Thanks to excellent farming practices and top-quality milk, Ed and Henry Parsons were recognized as "Massachusetts Outstanding Dairy Farmers." Their cows spend summer months on Mayval Farm's Turkey Hill pastures and winter months in a "free-stall barn" (which allows cows to come and go freely from the barn, lie down, and access food and water at will), eating only hay and corn grown on the Farm. When I looked at the Mayval Farm's website and reviewed photographs of their prized cows, they were like "pin-up girls," great looking and dignified big cows. The continually fluctuating milk prices spurred the Parsons to decide to use some of their milk for cheesemaking and to sell milk directly to customers, guaranteeing them a stream of fairly consistent revenue.

The Parsons' first generation of cheese includes *fromage blanc*, a soft cheese that they have flavored with black pepper, garlic, chives, basil, and, of course, maple syrup! I was surprised to learn that Mayval Farm is also making *skyr*, an Icelandic type of yogurt. I had eaten and loved *skyr* when I spent a lot of time in Scandinavia and skyr is beginning to appear in US markets.

The Parsons continue to work hard and look at ways to add value to their farm while keeping their standards of quality, resulting from traditional and best practices. In order to receive the state's viability grant, the Parsons had to guarantee a ten-year covenant on their 350 acres remaining a dairy farm. The Parsons have no intention of selling their land and are hoping that some of their children will return and farm. As Margie Parsons pointed out, "We're hoping that a couple of the children might take up a second career in farming and continuing the maple syruping. The Parsons have been on this land for 225 years and we aren't quitting now."

Before Noah Parsons III settled in the Pioneer Valley, Native Americans were making maple sugar in the region. It was Native Americans who taught the Europeans how to tap the trees and boil down the syrup. Native Americans cut a V shape in the maple trees, inserted a reed, and caught the sap in buckets, often made of birch bark. An early document recorded that a chief was honored with venison cooked in maple syrup. The Parsons are continuing a long and proud tradition of respecting the land and ingeniously utilizing its bounty.

Maple Syrup Pudding with Spiced Pecans

SERVES 4

Puddings are magical, smooth, a tasty tidbit. You wouldn't want to buy premade puddings at the store with all their stabilizers. When was the last time you had a homemade pudding? So why not learn to make pudding? It's about whisking. So simple. Treat yourself to this delightful maple-flavored pudding with just a hint of sweetness.

Equipment: Small ramekins or bowls

For the pudding:

3 tablespoons cornstarch

2 cups milk, preferably whole

½ cup maple syrup, preferably B grade for fuller flavor

Salt

For the pecans:

2 teaspoons sugar

½ cup pecans

½ teaspoon ground cinnamon

Nutmeg, freshly grated

Pinch of paprika

Pinch of salt

2 teaspoons unsalted butter

To prepare pudding: Put cornstarch in bowl and whisk in small amount of milk. Pour remaining milk into a small saucepan and add the cornstarch mixture slowly, whisking. Continue to whisk and add maple syrup and pinch of salt. Bring to simmer over medium heat, whisking frequently, as pudding starts to thicken. Remove from the heat and pour into four ramekins or little bowls. Cover with plastic wrap and chill to set.

To prepare topping: Put sugar and pecans in small skillet and stir till sugar is melted and pecans are browned, about 5 minutes. Sprinkle the pecans with cinnamon, several gratings of nutmeg, paprika and salt. Melt butter in pan and coat nuts. Place on a dry surface to cool.

To serve: Add some pecans on top of each ramekin of pudding.

Cricket Creek Farm

Owner: Jude Sabot; Manager: Topher Sabot
Williamstown

Cricket Creek Farm is a gorgeous spot. Once you see the adorable calves on their website, you'll rush to visit the farm. You don't have to be a child to have fun walking around the farm to visit with, and be amused and charmed by, the pigs and chickens and cows. Watching cheese being made is fascinating, and after you taste Cricket Creek's handcrafted cheeses, you will forever afterward cringe when you see uniform plastic-wrapped cheeses in the supermarket. Cricket Creek cheeses are aesthetically pleasing, making you want to cradle some of the round shapes, like my favorite, Maggie's Reserve, with its buttery brown textured rind. It's almost an artwork. There is also a Berkshire Bloom, soft Camembert-like cheese, which looks comfy enough to be a pillow. For the Warm Ricotta Cake winter farm recipe (later in this chapter), I'd buy one of Cricket Creek Farm's soft, fresh cheeses. You could try the plain cheese, one of the subtle flavors such as lavender and honey, or go wild with sun-dried tomatoes and kalamata olive! An Italian cheesemaker from southern Italy served as a mentor when the cheesemaking operation first began at Cricket Creek Farm. Soon the farm was creating its own distinct styles of cheese and they recently won two awards at the American Cheese Society competition.

You may need to use restraint when you visit the farm store, where you can purchase eggs, cheese, and meats from the farm. The store is licensed to sell raw milk from the family cows and eggs from the chickens. A major store feature is the fine meats—beef, pork, and veal. The animals are all pasture-raised, grass-fed. The cuts of meat range from pork and veal sausages to smoked ham and bacon, or special prime beefsteaks. Whatever meat you chose, you will know the animal

had a happy life on the farm. The cattle are rotated to various pastures in the summer and feed off hay in the fields in the winter. The pigs' diet is mostly whey, a cheese byproduct, but the pigs also get vegetable-scrap treats from the local co-op market and, since these pigs live outdoors, they can root around for bugs and plants too. If you live close by, you can order Cricket Creek Farm foods through a CSA order and Cricket Creek Farm products are carried in multiple stores in the Boston and New York regions, as well as in restaurants. If you plan on visiting the Canyon Ranch Resort and Spa, beware. The cheeses are on the menu there.

Cricket Creek Farm is a heroic story. When the largest dairy operation and farm in Williamstown, Massachusetts, was up for sale, the farm was destined for extinction and the land was likely to be subdivided and built to accommodate housing and commercial development. Owners of a neighboring property, Jude and Dick Sabot, came to the rescue when they bought the land and decided to maintain a working dairy farm in order to keep its Agricultural Protection status. The land was saved from ugly development and the farm converted from a larger agribusiness model to a smaller-scale farm where the animals would all be pastured—rotated and allowed to eat the natural pasture grasses instead of being kept in a barn and fed store-bought grains. Dick and Jude embarked on their multiyear master plan to convert the farm to using more sustainable methods and making artisanal cheese from their cows' milk. A family friend designed a New Zealand–style "swing parlor"—not for swing dancing in the living room, but an older cow-milking technique, now refined and revitalized, that allows the milker to work on eleven cows at once, and then swing to the other side of a central aisle and milk cows on the other side. A more efficient and cost-effective way to milk cows with less labor, this style of milking parlor is particularly suitable for smaller herds of cows and farms with a limited source of labor. Cricket Creek Farm is also experimenting with a new program to allow the baby calves to nurse from their mothers (healthier for babies but at a financial cost, since the mother's milk is going into the calves, not into milk sales).

Then, just two years after the Sabots bought the farm, in 2004, Dick Sabot died. After trying several different scenarios to keep the farm operating, the eldest son Topher came "home" in 2009 and took over the management of the farm. Farming is tough work under any circumstances, but converting a large dairy operation from a model that depleted the environment rather than restoring it is a particularly difficult challenge. Cricket Creek Farm, like other farms, has an active apprenticeship program, though the apprenticeship term is much longer on a dairy farm, where the cows and cheese operation is year-round (apprenticeships on veggie farms are usually just six months). A good friend, Michael Durante Jr., went off to apprentice at Cricket Creek Farm in the cold winter of 2013. I wondered how a successful college graduate who most recently created and then led a nonprofit, international project at Georgetown University in Washington, DC, would survive the mundane routines of rotating cows to different pastures, taking them hay in the winter, or hooking them up to milking stands in the parlor. Mike thrived and was grateful for the real-life training. He loved it and is continuing his career in sustainable farming with a goal of having his own farm.

A recent successful Kickstarter campaign surpassed its goal and will enable Cricket Creek Farm to renovate an existing stone structure into a community gathering space and rental-income property as well as invest in solar power to reduce electric costs. Every year Cricket Creek has been more successful as it becomes a farm that "honors its animals, respects the land, feeds its community and exemplifies a sustainable model for small-farm viability." Cricket Creek Farm is a story of a saved farm where Topher Sabot is putting down roots and starting his own family, where apprentices come to learn and go on to work on other farms or start their own. Life is good on Cricket Creek Farm for people, plants, and animals.

Pulled Pork with Roasted Tomatillo Salsa

SERVES 6

According to Michael Durante, a former dairy-farm apprentice at Cricket Creek Farm, the results of this recipe rely almost entirely on the quality of your pork. He advises that you purchase a pork butt or shoulder roast with a nice thick layer of fat on one side. Also, Mike suggests you look for a source of pork from hogs raised in a pasture and fed a diet of rich fats. Think: whey, milk, nuts, seeds. The pork will usually have a visible yellow tinge and produce a more flavorful result. Good-quality meat will make or break this recipe, according to Mike. The pigs at Cricket Creek Farm are fed this rich diet, producing just the right type of fat needed. Many farms in the Berkshires and Pioneer Valley are allowing pigs to free-range and eat all sorts of good stuff to make them healthy and tasty.

For the pork:

1 pork butt, about ½ pound per person
Salt
Butter or lard

For the salsa:

5 medium tomatillos
Spicy chile peppers such as 2–3 small jalapeños, poblanos, or habaneros (or a combination, to taste)
2–3 cloves peeled garlic
1 medium onion
Cilantro, to taste
Juice of 1 lime
Salt

To prepare pork: Salt the pork butt thoroughly and allow it to come to room temperature. In a heavy-bottom pan, like a cast-iron pan, sear the pork butt on all sides in butter or lard. Remove from pan and slow cook, in either an electric crock pot on low or in a dutch oven in the oven at 250°F, for at least an hour per pound or until you can break the roast apart easily with a fork. If there is a good layer of fat the roast should not dry out, but add a little water to the pot if it seems to be drying.

To prepare salsa: Roast the tomatillos, chiles, and garlic under a broiler. When charred, allow to cool then peel off the burnt pieces. Put all ingredients in a food processor and blend till smooth, or leave a bit chunky, depending on your taste.

To serve: Serve pork warm on tortillas with warm tomatillo salsa.

Farm Recipes

Carrot Salad with Cumin

SERVES 4–5

Simple Gifts Farm, Amherst

Located in Amherst, Simple Gifts Farm is a novel nonprofit entity. Precious farmland was saved by the Amherst community and folded into the North Amherst Community Farm, which then leases the land to farmers Jeremy Plotkin and Dave Tepfer and their families. The nonprofit status ensures that the land will be saved in perpetuity for organic farming, a wildlife corridor, and space for outdoor activities.

This recipe makes a great side dish, or you can top a bowl of greens with a big spoonful of this zesty salad.

¼ cup fresh lemon juice
2 tablespoons olive oil
½ teaspoon salt
½ teaspoon ground cumin
½ teaspoon ground coriander
2 cups coarsely shredded carrots (or sliced paper-thin
    with a food processor or mandoline)
2–4 tablespoons minced chives
1–2 teaspoons minced fresh mint
¼ cup currants
2 tablespoons toasted sesame seeds

In a medium bowl, combine the lemon juice, olive oil, salt, cumin, and coriander.

Add the carrots, chives, mint, currants, and sesame seeds and toss to combine.

You can eat this immediately, but it is even better if you allow the salad to marinate for an hour or more in the refrigerator.

Crusty Cassoulet with White Beans, Vegetables, Sausage, and Chicken

SERVES 8–10

Pekarski's Sausage, South Deerfield

Native American tribes living in Massachusetts and the French and English colonists each contributed their methods of slow cooking beans and salt pork to a dish that became popular throughout New England. Most people are familiar with Boston baked beans and Boston's nickname "Beantown." The recipe below combines the beans and pork tradition, flavors of a French cassoulet, and ingredients like local, organic sausage found at butchers like The Meat Market in the Berkshires, Sutter Meats in Northampton, or Pekarski's Sausage in South Deerfield.

When you try this easy version of the classic French cassoulet recipe, you will find the long, slow cooking of white beans and sausage makes for a hearty winter meal. Cook it in a large Dutch oven and heat up the leftovers another day. Flavor enhances with time.

My cassoulet recipe has become a perennial winter family favorite. It's ideal to make ahead for a ski trip. With a cover on the pot (or foil), reheat it at 300°F for 1 hour, adding liquid if necessary. It's also great for a dinner party. There is no last-minute preparation. Add a salad and you have a hearty winter meal.

Equipment: Large 8-quart cast-iron pan with top or Dutch oven or casserole dish

1½ pounds Great Northern beans (or substitute canned)

½ pound slab bacon, chopped in cubes

2 tablespoons butter

2 tablespoons olive oil

4 pounds chicken, cut into 8 pieces (or substitute duck or goose)

6 carrots, peeled and cut into quarters

1 medium onion, studded with 8 whole cloves

3 cups chicken stock, canned or homemade

2 bay leaves

5 medium onions, peeled

½ cup coarsely chopped celery leaves

1½ teaspoons salt

3 whole black peppercorns

3 clove garlic, crushed

1½ teaspoons finely chopped fresh thyme

1 teaspoon marjoram leaves, fresh or dried

1 teaspoon finely chopped fresh sage leaves

⅛ teaspoon ground black pepper

1 (1 pound) can peeled tomatoes

1 pound organic pork sausage, from butcher

To prepare the beans: Soak beans for 2 hours in 5 cups water. Do not drain. (Or use canned beans instead.)

Meanwhile prepare bacon and chicken: Cook bacon in heavy bottom saucepan till brown. Drain and set aside. Add butter and olive oil to the saucepan in which you cooked the bacon. Sauté all the chicken pieces at once or in two batches, depending on size of pan.

To make basic stew: Add half of carrots, 1 onion studded with whole cloves, chicken broth, bay leaves, onion, celery leaves, and spices—salt, peppercorns, garlic, thyme, marjoram, sage and pepper—to the beans and their liquid. Bring to boil, reduce heat, and simmer 1 hour. Add remaining three carrots; cook covered for 15 minutes.

To begin baking phase: Put beans, vegetables, and bacon into a large 8-quart cast-iron pan or dutch oven. Bake at 350°F, uncovered for 30 minutes.

For final two steps: Add the chicken to the bean and vegetable mixture. Add the can of tomatoes, including liquid from can. Place sausage in a circle on top of bean and chicken mixture. Cook 45 minutes, covered tightly. Bake uncovered 10 minutes or longer until a slight "crust" forms on the top. Add water if too dry.

Warm Ricotta Cake for Breakfast or Dessert

SERVES 4

Cricket Creek Farm, Williamstown

This simple, eggless cake is wonderful, paired with fresh or poached fruit, for a light dessert. Try the cake as a warm tasty surprise and serve it for breakfast. Yes, you may be accustomed to cereal and toast but follow the healthy example of many other parts of the world where cheese is served for breakfast. As a great source of protein, cheese gives your body the fuel for a good start to the day. My friend Gabriel brought this recipe home from a family in Umbria, Italy, where she stayed with them on their farm. Warm cheese—comfort food and a great energy source. Begin your day with joy. Try this recipe with fresh cheese from a farm like Cricket Creek Farm.

3 cups all-purpose flour
½ teaspoon baking soda
3 cups farm-fresh ricotta
2½ cups sugar
Zest of 2 lemons

To prepare cake: Whisk the flour and baking soda together in a small bowl. In a larger bowl, whisk the ricotta with the sugar and lemon zest until light and fluffy. Fold the dry ingredients into the ricotta mix.

To bake: Grease a 10-inch round cake pan and sprinkle 2 tablespoons of sugar all around the pan to coat it. Pour batter into prepared pan and bake in 350°F oven for 30–40 minutes until brown and puffed.

WINTER TOUR

Snow outside is just an excuse to sit by a fire and enjoy a meal, visit a holiday market, eat some exquisite chocolates, or relive the Norman Rockwell era as depicted in his painting *Main Street in Stockbridge*. Terrific restaurants welcome guests, and two iconic hotels of the region are extraordinarily cozy to visit in the winter. Blantyre dresses up a forty-foot tree in lights and offers winter sports and pampering service.

Main Street at Christmas, Stockbridge

The town of Stockbridge re-creates a Normal Rockwell painting of their Main Street, complete with exact placements of vintage cars. There is a Christmas market and various activities to fill in a whole day or two. Taste and buy foods at the Christmas Food Booth, tour historic houses, sing carols, ride in a horse-drawn wagon. Stories for adults and children are read at the town library and there are concerts and plays. Visit the nearby Norman Rockwell Museum.

MASS MoCA and Gramercy Bistro, North Adams

MASS MoCA is a visual and performing arts center in the country, located in a former vast industrial complex. The factory employed over four thousand workers who organized its own orchestra and co-op grocery store. When the textile and electric industries collapsed in North Adams, these brick structures were eventually transformed into a museum and music center. What a great place to get lost on some winter day, since there are tons

of art to appreciate or puzzle over. Dine at the Gramercy Bistro, located on the campus of MASS MoCA. Gramercy Bistro combines traditional dishes like paella and crab cakes with other more adventuresome offerings like sweetbreads and pork belly.

Stockbridge Cafe and Elm Street Market, Stockbridge

Stockbridge Cafe, formerly named Alice's Restaurant (made famous by Arlo Guthrie), is a favorite casual place for lunch. A block away, the Elm Street Market is a local spot with an old-fashioned luncheon counter and multiple refills of coffee.

Chocolate Springs, Lenox

Former chocolatier at the French Maison du Chocolat, Joshua Needleman, has opened his own specialty chocolate shop offering unique and exquisite European-style handmade chocolates, such as the Champagne Cognac truffles, made of a rare Champagne Cognac and dark chocolate, which *Time* magazine called "feathery light." Chocolate Springs is also a cafe with pastries, chocolate desserts, and rich hot chocolate—a fantastic place for brunch.

Elmer's Store, Ashfield

If you can, try to start one of your days in Ashfield at quirky Elmer's Store. Their famous breakfasts are served every morning from 8:00 to 12:00. The menu features local eggs and maple syrup and the various dishes are described in very amusing ways. The tummy-filling breakfasts are a great way to start a winter's day.

Mayval Farm, Westhampton

Stop here to buy your maple syrup for gifts and home use. For 225, years this farm has been in the same family. The farm follows traditional maple syrup–making methods and is one of the very best places to buy maple cream and maple butter. Mayval has a new farm store on the premises that offers cheese made on the farm and superior milk from their award-winning cows.

Sidehill Farm, Hawley

Take the time to drive up the hill to nearby Sidehill Farm and buy their terrific yogurt and raw milk for sale out of a beat-up refrigerator on the dirt farm road.

WINTER TOUR

The Porches, North Adams

When visiting MASS MoCA, enjoy staying at The Porches, listed on the register of the National Trust Historic Hotels of America and managed by the The Red Lion Inn's Main Street Hospitality Group. Porches was created from a group of repurposed row houses into a boutique hotel. There are, of course, porches on all the houses; the interior rooms are painted in interesting colors, from tangerine to soft yellow, and furnishings combine historic, retro, and contemporary styles. If you want to be cozy on a chilly day, order breakfast in bed and it will arrive in a large, silver-colored retro lunch box—one clever touch among many at this hotel. Visit during warmer seasons and enjoy that rocking chair on the front porch or swim in the heated swimming pool, hidden behind the historic façade of the hotel.

Spring

Small Plate

Smashed Peas in Endive

SERVES 5

It is hard for me to make it out of the garden with fresh peas. I want to shell and eat them right on the spot. I also don't want to cook them and lessen their exquisite flavor. Ah, spring and fresh peas.

Mint is a traditional herb used with peas and it works well to add a flavor to the peas. If you don't harvest too many fresh peas, putting them in endive leaves is a nice way to highlight them.

6 ounces fresh peas, shelled from 1 pound pea pods

6 sprigs of mint, very finely minced

1 ounce Parmesan cheese, finely grated

2–3 tablespoons olive oil

5 endive leaves, washed and dried (select leaves with no blemishes)

To prepare: Mash peas and mint with a fork. Mix in cheese and then the olive oil, a little at a time.

To serve: Place endive attractively on a platter and spoon mashed peas into each.

Tip: I sometime use Trader Joe's wasabi mayonnaise instead of Parmesan cheese, though I still add some grated cheese on top for flavor.

Appetizer

Wild Mushrooms on Toast

SERVES 4

Hopefully, you will have the opportunity to forage wild mushrooms when you are in the Pioneer Valley or Berkshires, either with a guide or on your own. Once you find these precious wild items, you will want to share and serve them to friends in a way that focuses only on the mushrooms. When I found chanterelles on my property, I created this recipe.

1 pound wild mushrooms, any type
2 tablespoons olive oil
2 tablespoons butter
2 cloves garlic, finely minced
2 sprigs fresh thyme, stems removed, leaves finely
    minced
½ lemon
1 baguette

To prepare: Slice mushrooms to a medium thickness. Place in a greased small roasting pan. Drizzle olive oil on top and sprinkle with small pieces of butter. Scatter garlic and thyme over the mushrooms. Roast for 10 minutes. Cook only till tender. Do not cook till mushrooms are shriveled. Just before serving, squeeze some lemon over mushrooms.

To prepare baguette: Cut baguette into thin slices and lightly toast on both sides.

To serve: Place mushrooms on baguette slices and serve while warm.

Bread

Scones with Chives

SERVES 4–6

My father was born in the United Kingdom and scones were always "regulars" in our house. I bake them many ways and especially enjoy using small wild cranberries or blueberries in them, but when someone suggested chives, I thought, "What an enlightened idea and ingredient." Little chives in scones just reek of springtime. You can buy chives in the market, but if you are like me, chives sprout in your spring garden.

My mother coated our scones with a cinnamon sugar mixture, which creates a bit of crust and crunch on the top (to contrast with soft interiors) and the egg white adds a bit of glisten and golden color.

For the dough:

2 cups unbleached white flour
2½ teaspoons baking powder
1 teaspoon salt
2 tablespoons sugar
2 tablespoons unsalted butter
½ cup cream or milk
2 egg yolks, well beaten
1 bunch chives, thin as possible

For the topping:

¼ teaspoon ground cinnamon
1 cup sugar
1 egg white, lightly beaten

To make dough: Place dry ingredients of flour, baking powder, salt, and sugar in mixing bowl. Put butter into the bowl with the flour and cut the mixture with two knives in criss-crossing fashion, or break up by hand until the butter is the size of small peas. Add cream and egg yolks and mix a few times. Cut chives with a sharp pair of scissors while holding chives over the bowl. Mix again until chives are distributed through the dough. Knead a few times until a soft dough forms.

To make scones: Put dough onto floured surface and knead until mixture holds together. Roll dough into an 8-inch circle (larger or smaller circle depending on the thickness of scones you desire). With a sharp, wide knife cut the dough into six sections, like pie slices. Place each one on a cookie sheet about 2 inches apart.

Prepare the cinnamon-sugar topping: Mix cinnamon with sugar in a small jar.

To coat scones: Using pastry brush, coat top of each scone with egg white and then sprinkle cinnamon sugar onto egg-white coating.

To bake the scones: Preheat oven to 425°F. Bake scones at 425°F for 12 minutes until light brown on top.

Soups

Chilled Green Melon Soup

SERVES 4

A dear friend, Anne Hussey, who is eighty-eight years old but has the appearance and spirit and intellectual curiosity of someone many years younger, lived in New York City for many years where she and her husband liked to entertain. He was a businessman with offices in the Empire State Building. With their third child, the Husseys decided to move to the suburbs, where they bought a beautiful barn, a former blacksmith shop that had been renovated and added onto by an architect. The chestnut-wood barn has a serene view of the Silvermine River in Connecticut, which formerly generated power for a dozen mills in the Silvermine area. Ann certainly knows food, having been the co-owner of the historic Roger Sherman Inn and Restaurant in New Canaan. When she served me this soup one hot summer day, I had to ask her for the recipe.

For the soup:

1 honeydew melon (or cantaloupe)
½ cup lime juice
4 teaspoon seeded, minced jalapeños, or ⅛ teaspoon sambal oelek, bottled red pepper flakes found in Asian markets
1 cup plain yogurt (Greek or regular style)
1¼ teaspoons salt
Ground pepper to taste, white or black

For the topping:

Slivered almonds, toasted (or purchase already toasted)
¼ cup chopped mint
1 ripe star fruit, cut crosswise into thin slices

To prepare: Cut the melon flesh from the rind, discarding seeds. Place melon, lime juice, jalapeños, yogurt, salt, and pepper in food processor and blend until smooth. Refrigerate until chilled.

To serve: Garnish each bowl of soup with some almonds and pinch of mint and, if you want to be super fancy, float a thin cross-section of the five-pointed fruit that makes the shape of a star.

Spinach Soup with Asian Flavors

SERVES 6

When spring comes, fresh spinach says, "Eat me." This recipe offers the quick option of pulling spinach right from the garden (or bag) and plunking the leaves into chicken broth to make soup. No dicing, no slicing—just sweet spinach leaves whole. Add glass noodles whose transparent color suggests lightness associated with spring. You can find these thin noodles, made from a starch like mung bean or cassava, in most supermarkets, and lemongrass and baby ginger are appearing in most Pioneer Valley and Berkshire farmers' markets. What a combination for a refreshing, light spring meal.

Soup:

1 (16 ounce) package glass noodles
3 lemongrass stalks
4 cloves garlic
4 inches ginger root, fresh and finely chopped
4 cups chicken broth
1 tablespoon vegetable oil
12 ounces fresh mushrooms, cremini, oyster, shiitake, or any other fresh mushroom sold in the farmers' market, coarsely chopped
1 red onion, chopped
14 ounces coconut milk (look for fat-free)
2 tablespoons red curry paste
3 tablespoons fish sauce
1 lime, juiced
1 bunch fresh, washed spinach (8 ounces)

Garnish:

½ bunch cilantro
1 lime, cut into wedges
1 jalapeño pepper, sliced into rings

To prepare noodles: Pour hot water over noodles and let them soak for few minutes, according to directions on package. Drain.

To make soup: Cut the tops off the lemongrass. Using only the white portion, chop into thin slices. Put sliced lemongrass, garlic, ginger, and chicken broth into large saucepan and bring to boil. Reduce heat and simmer 30 minutes.

In the meantime, five minutes before chicken broth mixture is ready, heat oil in a separate pan. Add the mushrooms and onion and cook 5 minutes till they are soft but not brown. Stir in coconut milk, red curry paste, fish sauce, and lime juice. When chicken broth has finished, add the chicken broth to the mushroom and onion mixture, then the strained glass noodles and spinach. Cook just until spinach wilts.

To serve: Divide into 6 bowls. Place a portion of cilantro on top of each bowl of noodles. Serve with lime wedges and fresh jalapeños for guests to add to their soup.

Salads

A Precious Ribbon-Zucchini and Tomato Salad with a Secret

SERVES 4–6

Haven't we all tried zucchini a thousand ways? No matter how many recipes I have experimented with, I have never been fond of this vegetable. That is, until I made this salad. The secret is cutting the zucchini with a mandoline slicer into thin, delicate ribbons. The zucchini becomes a whole new vegetable. Beware—there is a world of vegetable slicers out there. Don't be tempted to buy an expensive model. A simple board with a single sharp blade—for under $10—will cut the zucchini for this salad (and you'll love using it to cut potatoes, cucumbers, carrots, and other vegetables). My only warning is that the blade is razor sharp. Force yourself to stop before you are down to a minuscule piece. Eat the last bit and avoid bloody fingers, or buy a cut-resistant safety glove. Zucchini are prolific and relatively inexpensive so this salad with stretch your food budget while becoming a favorite.

For the salad:

4–6 medium zucchini (about 1½ pounds)
½ pound cherry tomatoes, multicolored if possible

For the dressing:

¼ cup extra-virgin olive oil
¼ cup lemon juice
Zest of 1 lemon
1 clove garlic, crushed
½ teaspoon salt
⅛ teaspoon red pepper flakes
2 tablespoons minced mint leaves
2 tablespoons basil (roll leaves into a tube-shape and cut in thin slices, called "chiffonade")
½ cup cured olives of your choice, optional

To prepare the salad: Cut the tops and tails off of the zucchini. Slice lengthwise on the mandoline, set at ⅛ inch. If you do not have a mandoline, slice in very thin rounds. Place the zucchini in a medium-size bowl.

To prepare the dressing: In another small bowl, whisk olive oil, lemon juice, zest, garlic, salt, and red pepper flakes. Pour over zucchini and massage into the ribbons. Let marinate for 15–20 minutes. Before serving, toss with the mint, basil, and lots of cherry tomatoes.

For a variation, add ½ cup olives and use oregano and cilantro in place of the mint and basil.

Jerusalem Artichoke Salad with Beans, Leeks, Hazelnuts, and Goat Cheese

SERVES 6

Are Jerusalem artichokes tied to Jerusalem as brussels sprouts are historically connected to Brussels? No, there is no connection. Plus, what are called Jerusalem artichokes aren't even artichokes. They are a type of tuber that was cultivated by Native Americans. The explorer Champlain, in fact, found them cultivated on Cape Cod when he arrived in 1605. When a friend said he had never tasted Jerusalem artichokes, I started to buy them at farmers' markets to experiment and create a favorite recipe. The name may be confusing, but once you start cooking Jerusalem artichokes, you will be enamored with their sweet, nutty flavor. Don't turn up your nose at Jerusalem artichokes. They can be truly delicious.

For the salad:

1½ pounds Jerusalem artichokes
2 tablespoons olive oil
2 large leeks, white portion only, finely sliced
1 (14 ounce) can white beans, like cannellini, drained
1 tablespoon finely minced fresh rosemary
1 tablespoon finely minced fresh sage, finely minced
Salt and pepper
Lettuce leaves

For the garnish:

½ cup hazelnuts, coarsely chopped or broken into pieces
2 ounces goat cheese, crumbled
1 tablespoon finely minced parsley

For the dressing:

1 tablespoon Dijon mustard
1 teaspoon whole-grain mustard
3 tablespoons olive oil
2 tablespoons balsamic vinegar
Salt and pepper

To prepare hazelnuts: If you can't buy hazelnuts without skins, you will need to toast the hazelnuts in a preheated oven at 350°F for 5 minutes. Spread them on a baking sheet in a single layer. Remove from oven and wrap in clean dish towel for a minute. Rub the nuts together till the skins fall off. Let cool. Chop coarsely or wrap them in another clean dishtowel and break them into pieces with a hammer.

To prepare artichokes: Peel artichokes and cut into thin slices. Sauté in olive oil until golden brown. Place top on sauté pan and cook on low heat for 25 more minutes.

Continue: Add leeks and cook until they are soft, about 6 minutes. Then add the white beans, rosemary, sage, pepper, and salt. Place artichokes, leeks, and beans in bowl, add the rosemary, sage, pepper, and salt. Mix two types of mustard, oil, vinegar, salt, and pepper in a jar, place lid on jar and shake. Dress with salad dressing. Add crumbled cheese.

To serve: Place lettuce leaves on small plates and spoon Jerusalem artichoke mixture on top of lettuce. Sprinkle with more crumbled cheese, parsley, and some hazelnuts.

Spring Salad with Lillian's Dressing

SALAD: SERVES 4

DRESSING: MULTIPLE SERVINGS

It wasn't too long ago that I was impressed when my brother and sister-in-law talked about rocket, a lettuce more commonly known as arugula. Now we are all familiar with arugula. It grows so easily in my garden that I can't eat it fast enough, so I use it to make pesto sauce. Now the rage is mâche and, to my delight, it proliferates in my garden as well. You'll find it at farmers' markets in the spring. Try it. Mâche has a nuanced, nutty, grassy taste. If you can't locate mâche, substitute watercress, radicchio, or frisée. Don't get salad burnout. Use arugula and mâche.

When I was growing up in the Boston area, Lillian was a neighbor who had a degree in home economics. She was an excellent cook, and her husband Reginald emphatically agreed.

For the salad:

¼ cup green pumpkin seeds, toasted

½ cup vegetable oil

8 ounces arugula

8 ounces mâche

½ cup feta cheese

1 Persian cucumber (small one with few seeds)

For the dressing:

1 teaspoon salt

½ teaspoon sugar

¼ teaspoon pepper

½ paprika

2 cloves garlic, finely minced

½ onion, finely minced

½ teaspoon dry mustard (or 1 teaspoon prepared mustard)

½ cup vegetable oil

¼ cup cider vinegar

½ teaspoon Worcestershire sauce

To prepare salad: Coat several cups green pumpkin seeds with oil and bake on aluminum foil in 350°F oven for 15–25 minutes. Set aside ¼ cup and save the remaining seeds in tight lidded jar for future use. Place arugula, mâche, crumbled feta cheese, and sliced cucumber in a bowl. Toss with Lillian's dressing and sprinkle with pumpkin seeds.

To prepare dressing: Put all ingredients in a jar, place lid on jar, and shake. Will keep indefinitely.

Entrees

Grilled Lamb Scottadito

SERVES 4–6

The Stanton brothers and Barber brothers of Great Barrington, a Berkshire town, know that animals are what they eat. Different breeds of animals and the chemistry of the soil that feed the plants that, in turn, are eaten by pastured or free-range animals impart distinctive tastes. At first terroir was applied to wines, then to coffees, but now there is talk of the terroir of meat. If you can, buy lamb for the following recipe at The Meat Market. If not, search around for your own source.

After a cold winter, everyone is excited at the prospect of emerging new tender herbs and being able to get outside to grill again. This recipe will elevate your grilling success as it uses an unusual pesto, a distinctive combination of arugula, mustard, and dandelion. Dandelion greens are now appearing in my Giant supermarket, which is not a gourmet store. If you can't find it, substitute watercress, chicory, or baby spinach.

This is definitely a slow-food dish because it combines fresh, healthy foods cooked in a time-honored tradition that calls for bringing together "community." Grilling spring lamb is a special event for friends and family. *Scottadito* in Italian means "scorched fingers," so eat it while it is hot!

For the lamb:

Lamb—approximately 2½ pounds, about 2–3 racks of lamb (plan on 2 ribs per person)
Salt and pepper
2 lemons, cut into wedges

For the marinade:

4 juniper berries
4 peppercorns
½ cup olive oil or lard*
½ cup dry white wine
2 bay leaves torn into small pieces
2 cloves crushed garlic

For the Spring Herb Pesto:

4 cups (4 ounces) arugula leaves, cleaned
6 cups (6 ounces) mustard greens, cleaned and destemmed
2 cups (3 ounces) dandelion greens, cleaned and destemmed
½ cup raw almonds
1 cup extra-virgin olive oil
½ cup lemon juice
2 cloves garlic, peeled
1–1½ teaspoons salt, to taste

To prepare the marinade: Crush the juniper berries and peppercorns either in a mortar with pestle or folded in a piece of fabric such as a dishtowel, using a heavy rolling pin. Whisk olive oil, white wine, bay leaf, crushed juniper, peppercorns, and garlic in a small bowl. Brush the marinade over the lamb on all sides and then marinate the lamb for 12 hours or overnight in the refrigerator.

*If you are using lard, warm the lard so that it softens but doesn't melt. Stir in the wine, spices, and garlic to make a paste, which should be rubbed into the lamb.

To prepare the pesto: Place all ingredients in blender, puree. Add more olive oil to get texture you prefer.

To prepare the lamb: Take lamb out of refrigerator 20 minutes before cooking to bring it to room temperature and ensure even cooking. Remove the lamb from the marinade and pat dry. Add salt and pepper.

To prepare grill or grill pan: Heat until medium hot* and grill the lamb about 3–4 minutes on each side, basting once with the leftover marinade. The lamb will continue to cook once you have removed it from the grill, so don't overcook the meat. You want the center to be a light pink.

*My method for testing the temperature is to hold my hand over the grill and count in seconds to determine how long I can keep my hand over the coals: 1–2 seconds is scorching hot, 2–4 seconds is hot, 4–6 seconds is medium hot, and anything longer than that is medium cool.

To serve: Serve lamb immediately with a spoonful of the spring herb pesto and a wedge of lemon.

Spring Chicken and Vegetables

SERVES 6

Suddenly it is spring. We feel like being outside and eating lighter meals. This one-bowl meal is one of my go-to recipes. Feel free to alter it. I add whatever vegetables I have in my garden, like spring peas or mâche. Pasta and pesto are the key ingredients but the dish can change depending on what you add (bacon, perhaps?) and what type of pasta you use. Save some of the pesto sauce you make from the various pesto recipes in the summer season section.

1 pound pasta (rigatoni is good because it catches the sauce)

2 cups chicken, from breast or thigh, cooked and cut into bite-size pieces

2 cups baby spinach or arugula

⅓ cup pesto, add more to taste (see summer season pesto recipes)

½ cup crumbled goat cheese

½ cup walnut pieces

Red pepper flakes

To prepare: Cook pasta in boiling salted water according to directions. Drain but save water. Drop spinach or arugula in hot water until it is limp. Quickly drain and add to pasta. Add chicken. Toss pasta with pesto sauce. (I like a lot of pesto but you should be respectful of your guests.) While pasta is still hot, add the cheese, which should melt and coat some of the pasta. Add the walnut pieces and as many pepper flakes as you like.

Supper Eggs with Ramps and Fiddleheads

SERVES 2

Ramps and fiddlehead ferns grow wild in the Berkshires and Pioneer Valley. They can't be commercially grown, so they reach the markets through professional foragers and therefore are a bit costly, though well worth the price since they are a rare and delicate treat in the spring. The season is short, so you shouldn't go broke. Once when friends were visiting, I had us all picking fiddlehead fern fronds on a path behind the Berkshire house, counting up all the dollars I was saving by this foraging endeavor. Ooops, they weren't the great fiddlehead ferns I had picked in Japan or bought in the market. Now I just stick to the local farmer, who will have them in the markets.

Ramps are in the allium family, a mix of onion with a gentle garlic overtone. Honor these special spring vegetables by making a supper meal out of them. I call this dish supper because the slight garlic taste seems better in the evening with a glass of wine than at breakfast with coffee. Ramps are special enough by themselves, but since fiddlehead ferns are also in season why not combine the two? To add an exotic taste to these local foods, I have added tortilla as a base, topped with avocados and black beans.

3 tablespoons butter

1 bunch ramps

1 pint fiddlehead ferns

4 eggs

2 large whole-wheat tortillas

1 cup black beans, drained from can

½ avocado

¼ cup sour cream

Sprinkle of sriracha sauce

To prepare the vegetables: Melt butter in saucepan and sauté ramps and fiddleheads for about 3 minutes at medium heat. Remove from pan. Add more butter and fry 4 eggs to your preference—soft or dry. Remove from pan. Wipe pan dry with paper towel or cloth. Turn heat to high and toast tortilla on both sides for 1 minute till each side is lightly toasted.

To serve: Place 1 tortilla on each plate, 2 eggs, and ramps and fiddleheads. On the side, add some black beans, avocado slices, and sour cream. Lightly sprinkle on chile sauce—enough to add spark but not enough to overpower the delicate taste of the ramps and fiddleheads.

Mushroom and Spinach Ramequin

SERVES 4–6

I have a stained 4 x 6 recipe card with this recipe taped onto it—with an asterisk and a handwritten note, "excellent." It seems like a recipe my mother passed on to me, but I see on the Internet that the recipe is very close to a "ramequin forestier" that Julia Child demonstrated on a television show. I love soufflés and quiche and this timeless recipe falls into the same "fluffy, puffed up" egg category, yet it is easier to make than a soufflé (no fear of egg whites not inflating) and less fattening than quiche since it doesn't have a butter-pastry crust. Make sure your family or guests are sitting down before you take this dish out of the oven. It looks dramatic when it is warm, but falls as it cools. The cheese and butter on the top turn a golden brown. I like to add baby spinach to the filling if I am not serving the dish with a salad. Not only is this dish attractive, it is sensationally delicious.

Ramequin is a term for a style of French cooking container that is white, fluted around the outside, and ovenproof. It can be small, such as those used for individual crème brûlées or large, like those for soufflés. You may use any ovenproof container that is 9 inches in diameter with 2-inch sides.

For the filling:

1 cup fresh mushrooms, preferably cremini, or a mix of
    your favorites, finely chopped
1 tablespoon minced shallots or scallions
1 tablespoon butter
1 tablespoon olive oil
½ cup flour
4 tablespoons heavy cream
½ teaspoon salt
¼ teaspoon pepper
Pinch ground nutmeg

For the roux:

½ cup all-purpose white flour
2 cups milk
4½ tablespoons butter
4 eggs
1⅓ cups coarsely grated swiss cheese
3 cups baby spinach (3–4 ounces)

To prepare the filling: Sauté mushrooms and shallots in butter and olive oil till mushrooms start to brown. Sprinkle in the flour and stir for 2 minutes to cook the flour. Remove from heat and gradually pour in the cream. Stir till it thickens. Add salt, pepper, and nutmeg.

Make the roux: Place flour in heavy-bottom saucepan over medium heat. Gradually add the milk while beating with a wire whisk. Stir constantly till mixture thickens and comes to boil. Take off the heat and whisk in 3½ tablespoons of butter, then the eggs, one by one. Stir in 1 cup cheese and spinach.

To assemble: Put half of the egg-milk mixture into the baking dish. Spread mushrooms on top and cover with the remaining mixture. Dot the top with 1 tablespoon of butter and ⅓ cup cheese.

To bake: Bake 25–30 minutes until risen and golden brown. Serve immediately because eggs will fall like a soufflé.

Desserts

Sour Cherry Pie

SERVES 8

One of my first experiences with a cherry pie occurred on George Washington's birthday when I won a cherry pie for being the thousandth customer at a new store. Never having won anything before, I brought it home, but no one would eat it because it was full of sugar, cornstarch and lots of red dye.

Then I was introduced to sour cherries. There are lots of old heritage cherry trees in the Berkshires and Pioneer Valley. These fruits should be cherished as cherry tree blossoms are in Japan. The season for the fruit is short. These sour cherries can be smallish and some trees only bear fruit in alternate years. Plus there is the challenge of picking the cherries before the birds get them— just when they are ripe but not too ripe! One certainly wouldn't go to the work of pitting them if it weren't worth the effort. Thankfully, fresh cherries, right from the tree, beat any canned cherries. These little babies are packed with flavor. Look for them at the farmers' market.

I have my own sour cherry tree, and a food memory branded in my heart is the gratitude of two male friends who thoroughly enjoyed eating my cherry pie outside on my porch one gorgeous June day. Even I admitted it was "quite divine."

Equipment: 8- or 9-inch pie pan

For the pie crust:
2 cups flour
1 teaspoon salt
1½ sticks unsalted butter
½ cup cold water, with ice cubes

For the pie filling:
4–6 cups cherries
1 cup cherry juice
⅓ cup cornstarch
1 cup sugar, white

To make the pie dough: Place flour and salt in a medium-size bowl, add butter, and chop it into size of peas, using knife in each hand or working it quickly with your fingers. Drip cold water onto the flour-butter mixture and gather till it holds a ball shape. Knead two to four times until flour and butter seem fairly well blended. Divide dough in half and chill in refrigerator several hours.

To roll out the pie dough: Sprinkle flour on a bread board or countertop and roll out half of the dough into a circle large enough to fit into your pie pan. Cut circle with a knife and fold the dough in half. Gently pick it up and place it in a greased pie pan. Unfold to fill the pan with about ½ inch extending over the edge. Wet the edges.

To make filling: Pit the cherries with cherry pitter. Save any juice from the cherries or pulverize a few cherries in a food processor and strain till you have 1 cup juice. Combine the cornstarch, sugar, and cherry juice in a small saucepan and cook over medium heat until the mixture thickens. Add cherries and put filling into pie shell.

Make top crust of pie: Roll the second ball of dough and cut a circle large enough to extend over edges of pie pan. Fold dough in half and gently place on top of pie filling. Cut any excess. Roll edges of top layer of dough under the bottom layer. Pinch to seal. Press a fork into the edge to seal and create a decorative design. Prick fork through dough in a few places to allow steam to escape.

To add an extra touch: If you feel creative, cut out a round cherry shape and two leaves from the leftover dough. Roll a little piece of dough to make a stem. Brush some water onto the top of the pie crust and adhere the cherry, stem, and leaves. Or for an easier, fun look, before you place dough on pie, use a small round canapé cutter to cut circles. They will allow a "sneak preview" of the gorgeous red color of your cherry pie.

Note: If you don't have a cherry pitter, you can make your own. Use the cone-shaped top of a cake decorating tip. Or take a thin, inexpensive metal fork and bend each outer tine backwards with needle-nose pliers and then make a small hook on the two inner tines. You will be able to insert this into the bottom end of the cherry to reach in and pull out the pit.

Caraway Seed Cake

SERVES 8–10 (BEST IN SMALL SLICES)

Since the British were early settlers in Massachusetts, there is still a strong British influence on foods in the Pioneer Valley and Berkshires, such as this seed cake recipe. My mother used to bake this cake and now, suddenly, that caraway seed cake is making a comeback. It is a great travel cake since it has no frosting! The caraway seeds add a slightly crunchy texture and the buttery taste melts in your mouth. It's a sweet-savory cake and a good option if you aren't a fan of sweet cakes. I like to bake the cake in a round cake pan, but use a loaf pan if you are planning to slice it as part of a proper English tea.

Equipment: 8-inch round cake pan or 8 x 4-inch loaf pan lined with parchment paper

1¾ cups white flour, unbleached, all-purpose
1 teaspoon baking powder
½ teaspoon salt
½ pound (2 sticks) butter, room temperature
1 cup sugar
1 teaspoon vanilla extract
1 large lemon, grated zest
3 eggs, lightly beaten
2 tablespoons caraway seeds, or to taste

To prepare: Whisk flour, baking powder and salt in a bowl. Using an electric mixer (hand or stand) cream the butter until soft, then gradually add the sugar and beat until the mixture becomes light and fluffy. Add vanilla and lemon zest, then add the eggs and mix until the mixture is thoroughly combined. With the mixer on low, gradually add the flour mixture. Stir in the caraway seeds with a rubber spatula.

To prepare cake pan: Grease and flour the baking pan.

To bake: Bake at 350°F for about 30 minutes until center is firm and sides start to pull away from pan. Cool 5 minutes before removing cake from pan and cooling again on wire rack. Cool completely before serving.

Restaurants

Old Inn on the Green

Executive Chef: Peter Platt
Co-owners: Peter Platt and Meredith Kennard
New Marlborough

This historic tavern, with its candlelight-only interior dining, could be saccharine and phony. Instead, the Old Inn on the Green has rightly earned top honors for several reasons. At the top of the list is Chef Peter Platt's daring cuisine using local foods in original ways full of delicious flavors. The Inn is fortunate to be located in a remarkable setting in an unspoiled New England village surrounded by trees, fields, and a few other pristine period structures with soothing views across the grass to hills in the distance. The inn is almost unaltered from its eighteenth-century tavern origins. It retains its history in several dining areas, all furnished with antique period tables and Windsor-style chairs. There are no pseudo-colonial touches like other "quaint" inns around New England. If it wasn't there originally, the owners haven't tried to replicate it. One particular touch that I found inspired is the use of natural dried materials like bark, seed pods, bare branches, or simple wire rings used subtly and discreetly to add texture and intrigue on the porch or in the corner of a room. These are a quiet decorative touch, belonging to the realm of art, not some trite imitation of the past. The simplicity and elegance, as well as the setting and cuisine, make the Inn a distinctive experience.

The inn dates to 1760, when it was a stagecoach stop where guests ate and slept before continuing on their journey. The original structure with double porches on the façade, downstairs and up, still serves dinner and offers rooms for guests with its eleven guest rooms in the original inn and an adjacent building on the property. Whether coming from the east or west, you reach the inn via country roads that wind up and down gentle hills dotted with farms until you reach New Marlborough. The inn sits at the top of the hill facing the small village green along with a nineteenth-century Friends Meeting House and a few other historic houses. I felt as if I had been picked up and dropped into paradise when I rented a small cottage across the village green from the inn with only an exquisitely crafted stone wall and road to separate me from the main building. In the spring and summer seasons, I watched the trees and lawn around the inn turn shades of green so lush I wanted to pinch myself to be sure the pleasure was real and not a dream. The outside dining area would open and I could go over to the inn for a drink or dinner, watch the sun, and inhale the views. In the fall, the inn is set against a backdrop of red and yellow leaves.

Yet it is the winter season that is, in many ways, the most magical time at the inn. Staff tend real wood fires that burn in each dining room, and with the sole lighting source being candles (no electric lights), the furniture, people, and food are all bathed in a soft glow. The warmth of the fires, light, and food creates a cozy haven from the cold outside. Ruth Reichl, the former editor of *Gourmet* magazine, wrote a review saying, "In the wintertime, there may be no more romantic dining than this aptly named inn, warmed by the roaring fireplaces and lighted entirely by candles. On a clear, cold night, when the air is so crisp that it crackles, nothing is as nice as walking into this golden welcome."

Executive Chef Peter Platt cooks with a sophisticated elegance. He uses traditional French cooking techniques and traditional ingredients—fresh and local—but he layers his cuisine with an innovative American approach. Peter had a short ride to the top with just three phases. He graduated from Williams, the excellent local private college, and went straight to the Parker

House in Boston. The hotel restaurant is famous for its Parker House rolls (always a Thanks-giving favorite in my family) and its famous guests, from the nineteenth-century literary talent of Emerson and Thoreau to sports celebrities such as Ted Williams and Babe Ruth. From the Parker House, Platt was hired as sous chef at Wheatleigh (profiled in the summer season section of this book) where he worked for fourteen years and rose to become executive chef. In 2002 he was hired away as the executive chef of the Old Inn on the Green. Peter's wife Meredith came to work at the inn, too.

Before her tenure at the inn, Meredith's experiences in the Berkshires involved working at two institutions that I admire. For several years, Meredith held the position of director of the Chatham House, a group home for mentally disabled adults, one of several model projects for the men-tally and severely physically disabled in the Berkshires. Then Meredith moved on to the Hancock Shaker Village (profiled in the summer season section). First she worked as the assistant farm and garden manager and then assumed the title of general manager. As head gardener, her responsi-bilities included two period gardens, Shaker medicinal herb gardens, all the field crops for feeding the animals, and the Shaker heirloom seed-saving program, in which varieties of seeds were preserved and packaged for museum use and retail sale.

Then-owners of the Inn, Bradford Wagstaff and Leslie Miller, greatly respected Peter's fine cooking and the contributions of Meredith, a highly capable manager and gardener. They couldn't imagine better owners, and negotiated the sale of the inn, including the dining room and lodging facilities, to Peter and Meredith. In 2005, Peter and Meredith finalized the purchase of the Old Inn on the Green and immediately established themselves as offering the highest level of dining and lodging, not just in the Berkshires but at a national level. The inn has received the highest acco-lades from national publications and rating services like Zagat.

The inn offers dinner daily with the exception of Tuesday, when the inn is closed. Besides an a la carte menu offered every night except Saturday and holidays, the inn highlights some of Chef Platt's extraordinary specialties with a Chef's Tasting Menu. On Saturday night, following a longstanding tradition, the inn offers a special prix fixe with four courses and nine entree choices. On Wednesday, Thursday, and Sunday, guests can dine on another more casual prix fixe. I like to put myself in Peter Platt's hands with his prix-fixe menus. I know he has selected what is local and fresh from his best sources to create an innovative and delicious tasting experience.

Since 2004, Peter and Meredith have also owned and operated the Southfield Store, close by in Southfield. The Southfield Store had operated as a general store from around 1907 until 2001, when it was sold and converted to a cafe. Now, in addition to a cafe, it contains a commercial baking kitchen created to accommodate the combined baking needs of the Southfield Store, the Old Inn on the Green, and catering engagements.

Today Southfield Store is a cafe and coffee bar, where breakfast and lunch are served year round. The second home–owners who live nearby have tried hard to keep word from spreading about the terrific brunches, but they have become very popular since, as one vacation homeowner told me, "It's hard to keep a light hidden under a basket." Shelves of fine grocery products make it hard to leave without making some type of purchase. The temptations include a wide selection of local and international cheeses, cured meats, wine, beer, and spirits, as well as kitchenware and gifts. In the summer months, it is possible to have dinner at the store Thursday through Sunday. The Mexican-born chef at the store offers a wonderfully innovative Oaxacan cuisine. The web-site declares, "No cheesy burritos here. Rather, the simple, clean flavors of the region with family recipes like Poblano Chile Rellenos stuffed with locally foraged mushrooms." Whether you visit the more casual store or the distinctive Old Inn on the Green, you will be surprised at the gems hidden in the Berkshire Hills. The Old Inn on the Green is a rare New England experience that warrants a special trip to Massachusetts.

Herb-Roasted Chicken Breast with Grain and Spring Vegetable Salad, Hen-of-the-Woods Mushrooms, and Charred Red Pepper Sauce

SERVES 4

Recipe by James P. Carr, Chef de Cuisine, Old Inn on the Green

For the red pepper sauce:

4 red bell peppers

2–3 teaspoons full-flavored oil, such as olive oil

2–3 garlic cloves, roasted

2–3 teaspoons apple cider vinegar

Big pinch of pimentón (substitute paprika if necessary)

Salt and pepper to taste

For the chicken:

4 chicken breasts with the skin, preferably "Statler" or "airline" style (see note below)

Salt and pepper

2–3 tablespoons neutral oil, such as canola

1 tablespoon butter

2 garlic cloves, peeled and crushed

3–4 sprigs of herbs (thyme, rosemary, sage)

For the salad:

2 cups cooked grains (barley, wheat berries, or Khorasan wheat, usually listed by brand name Kamut)

1 cup peas, shelled and blanched (frozen peas are fine)

2–3 teaspoons chives, chopped or snipped

Salt and pepper

Flavored oil (smoked, mushroom, or garlic) to taste

Lemon juice to taste

1 cup hen-of-the-woods mushrooms

Sprig of thyme

20 asparagus spears

2 medium leaves of kale or chard

To prepare charred red pepper sauce: Grill the four peppers on high heat until the skin is completely black and the flesh is soft. (Oven roasting is acceptable but doesn't produce same char.) Cool, slit, remove seeds, and peel half of the skin off three of the peppers. Skin the fourth pepper, dice and reserve for salad. Put the three partially peeled peppers in bowl of food processor, add flavored oil, roasted garlic cloves, apple cider vinegar, pimentón, and salt and pepper, and process until sauce is smooth and flecked with charred bits. Taste and adjust seasoning. Sauce will have a slightly acid taste and yet sweet from the peppers and smoky from the char.

To prepare the roast chicken: Season both sides of chicken breasts with salt and pepper. Heat canola oil in sauté pan and gently place chicken skin-side down and sauté for few minutes till skin is brown and crispy. Place butter, garlic, and herbs in a roasting pan, add the chicken crispy skin-side up, and roast for 15 minutes in 375°F pre-heated oven. Reserve cooking juices.

To prepare grain salad: Combine the cooked grains, peas, reserved diced peppers, chives, salt, pepper, fla-vored oil, and lemon juice to taste in medium-size bowl. Sauté the mushrooms with a sprig of thyme, a little garlic, and a pinch of salt. Grill, blanch, or steam the asparagus until just tender. Wilt the greens with a little vegetable stock and a pinch of salt.

To assemble: Pile a little mound of the grain salad on a plate and top with the asparagus, mushrooms, and greens. Make a swoosh of red pepper sauce on the plate, like a landing strip for the chicken. Place the chicken on the sauce, spoon over the cooking juices, and enjoy.

Note: Statler or airline breast chicken is the name for a boneless chicken breast with the first joint of the wing attached. If you can't find a butcher to prepare it, watch this YouTube video: www.youtube.com/watch?v=Row4H-HA5MAQ. A regular chicken breast is fine for this recipe.

Roasted Red Beet Tarte Tatin

SERVES 12

Equipment: 12 small aluminum tart pans

2 large beets
1 cup goat cheese (chèvre)
Small bunch of chives, finely chopped
Small bunch of parsley, finely chopped
¼ cup olive oil
1 cup white sugar
¼ pound (1 stick) unsalted butter
1 package puff pastry

To prepare beets: Trim off beet tops. Wash and individually wrap beets in foil, place in roasting pan, and roast in 350°F oven until a knife easily pierces beets, about 1–1½ hours. Cool and peel off skins.

To prepare cheese: Blend herbs into cheese, adding olive oil a little bit at a time to help integrate herbs.

To make caramel: Combine sugar and butter in a medium saucepan over medium to high heat and stir with a whisk occasionally until caramel turns a light brown color. Be careful—caramel is extremely hot. Pour hot caramel into a 2- to 4-cup Pyrex measuring cup to make it easier to pour into tart shells. It also stops the caramel from continuing to darken.

To prepare for baking: Pour hot caramel into tart pans to just cover bottom. Caramel will harden, which is fine. (This can be done up to a day in advance.) Slice beets about a half inch thick and cut the slices into circles, using cookie cutter, the same diameter as the bottom of the tart pan. Add beet rounds to tart pans, on top of the caramel. Cut rounds of puff pastry the same diameter and place the rounds on top of the beets. Bake at 425°F until pastry is brown and the caramel is bubbling, about 10 minutes.

To assemble: Turn out beet tarts onto plates while still hot (this can be a little messy and dangerous because caramel is liquid and hot). Pastry should be on the bottom and the beet on the top after the tarts have been plated. Garnish each tart with a spoonful of the herbed goat cheese and serve immediately.

Blue Heron

Executive Chef: Deborah Snow
Co-owners: Deborah Snow and Barbara White
Sunderland

Deborah Snow, executive chef of the Blue Heron restaurant, is one of the most outstanding chefs and restaurant owners in the Berkshire and Pioneer Valley region. Her food is really divine: delicious, with great taste combinations, elegant yet robust flavors and nice presentation.

Deborah's cuisine is fantastic, but it is Deborah—the person—who really makes the restaurant. This is one classy woman. She led a fascinating life in her former careers. Her life experiences with food and people deeply influence the restaurant. An activist with enlightened politics, Deborah is strong, kind, and caring. Love is part of the vocabulary she uses in describing the restaurant's philosophy, "Our food is a reflection of my grandmother's teachings: Eat fresh and eat the season, and all of it with love. Love your food, love your farmer." Deborah told a touching story of how encounters with a certain customer taught her to be more humble. "Food allows me to connect with almost anyone," she said.

The first restaurant Deborah founded in 1997 with her partner Barbara White was in Montague at the former 1844 Grist Mill, which also houses the Montague Book Mill (whose memorable slogan is "All the books you don't need in a place you can't find"). Deborah and Barbara had operated their restaurant for six years when they realized it was time to expand into a space and location with more options. By coincidence, over many cups of coffee in a coffee shop owned by the Pierce Brothers (who are profiled in the fall season section), Barbara and Deborah dreamed about and then planned their new restaurant, Blue Heron, which they opened in 2004.

To house Blue Heron, Deborah and Barbara bought the former Sunderland Town Hall. This brick town hall structure, dating from 1868, had previously served as town offices, school, library, town theater, and a basement "holding pen" for those who might have had a wee too much to drink. Over the years, the library and school spun off into their own buildings and eventually the town hall was vacant. Deborah and Barbara retained the historic bones and beauty of the original structure while tastefully and adaptively converting the space to a restaurant, with the help of a local architectural firm, Turtle Island Designs. Though not required by historic regulations to make this change, they restored to the façade its original Italianate porch, replacing a Colonial Revival porch that had been added at the height of Colonial Revival fever in the early twentieth century.

Barbara and Deborah preserved the pressed-tin walls. Rather than tear out or subdivide the Lincoln Theater, complete with stage, curtain, and seating area on the second floor, they used visual dividers to accommodate large or small parties. The grandeur of the Lincoln Theater remains. Simultaneously, the space allows for intimate dining. A separate room on the second floor is perfect for special small gatherings. On the main level, the former town offices have been converted to a commercial kitchen. A bar and lounge now replace the former gymnasium and the remaining area is carved into several seating areas. The furnishings and settings are elegant but somehow casual at the same time.

The colors are warm and attractive—shades of Persian orange, deep purples, and forest green. (It may not sound like an appealing color combination, but they are colors typical of the 1860s. As the former director of large restoration projects, I was familiar with similar historic colors and admired Deborah and Barbara's courage in using period-appropriate colors.) What truly impressed me was that the Blue Heron restoration project was completed on time and on

budget, an example of Barbara and Deborah's excellent management capacities, efficiency, and people skills.

It was evident that Deborah really knew her providers when she detailed the various farmers and food producers who source the restaurant. Deborah had researched and personally visited the Pioneer Valley's farms many times. She was aware of who grew the tastiest tomatoes and best grass-fed beef. It was more than "fad-talk." Deborah grew up with ideals and aspirations for making the world a better place, and her commitment to the very best sustainably raised, organic ingredients for the health of her customers and the planet is genuine.

The restaurant is popular with the local population, educated locavores who appreciate the excellent cuisine and wines at the restaurant. For people who live in and around Sutherland, Deborah and Barbara offer cooking classes on a regular basis, as well as by special request. Blue Heron is also a big draw for the parents, students, faculty, and trustees associated with the Five Colleges (Amherst, Mount Holyoke, Smith, UMass, and Hampshire) and private schools like Deerfield Academy and Eaglebrook, which are all located in the Pioneer Valley. The restaurant offers specials for parents' weekends and graduations. The people who travel to the Five College area are grateful for the presence of Blue Heron. Naturally it's not a surprise to find fine dining in the Pioneer Valley, which boasts twenty-five feet of prime topsoil in many locations and is the home to numerous organic farms, raising wonderful food. But it is Deborah's cuisine, which is equal to what some parents and trustees are accustomed to in food meccas like northern California or New York City, that attracts them and generates return visits.

It was quite a leap for Deborah and Barbara to purchase, design, equip, and plan an entire restaurant. Both women had always loved to cook but their career paths had taken them in other directions for the first halves of their lives. For a time, Deborah worked for Olivia Records, a women's collective devoted to producing women's music as a feminist-run business. With her photographic talent, Deborah was selected as a UN photographer in 1982 to document seniors in all parts of the world for the UN Year of the Aging. It was hard for a woman to compete with mostly male photographers in those days, yet Deborah reached the top with a major exhibit at the UN.

Then, ironically, having achieved this goal, Deborah wondered exactly where her career as a photographer would take her and decided to turn to her love for food. Her international travels had educated her taste buds and she was interested in creating "approachable food with love in it." First she worked at a restaurant and then as a food manager at Bread and Circus in Boston. When Deborah moved to the Pioneer Valley, she operated a catering business for Amherst College and Northfield Mount Hermon School, a college and independent school in the heart of Pioneer Valley, where she met Barbara.

When Barbara White came to the area, she took a position as a campus dean and director of parent programs at Northfield Mount Hermon School. Then Barbara and Deborah founded a catering business. This all led to their founding two restaurants. Barbara was an integral part of Blue Heron until her recent retirement. She says, "It isn't as if I have truly retired, but I do have a bit more free time and can even cook at home."

Obviously these women bring rich and varied experiences to all aspects of managing the business and relating to staff, clients, and food producers and vendors. I ended the interview with a great "activist" conversation with them about everything from tomato pie and hake to the role of agribusinesses like Sysco, Tyson, JBS, Cargill, and Monsanto. Deborah remarked, "Food has a lot of power to highlight the harm of these corporations and make the public aware of why we need to focus on sustainability as a way of life." Blue Heron is a symbol of how Barbara and Deborah hope to bring about change in their own humble way. They are smart co-owners of the Blue Heron and Executive Chef Deborah serves their customers delicious food in a classic historic setting.

Seared Scallops with Le Puy Lentils

SERVES 6

Chef Snow has organized this recipe to prepare two of the steps on the day before you are serving this dish. You can, of course, do everything on the same day.

For the mascarpone cream:

½ cup dry white wine

2 tablespoons finely chopped shallots

¼ cup whipping cream

¼ cup mascarpone cheese

1 teaspoon finely grated lemon peel

½ teaspoon fresh chives, minced

For the cider reduction:

2 cups apple cider

1 cup cider vinegar

½ cup minced shallots

For the lentils:

6 whole cloves

1 medium onion, peeled

6 cups water

1½ cups French green lentils (lentilles du Puy)

2 bay leaves

6 slices thick-cut applewood-smoked bacon,
   cut crosswise ¼ inch thick

1 teaspoon thyme, finely chopped

For the scallops:

6 tablespoons butter

18 sea scallops, patted dry

Salt and pepper

2 tablespoons olive oil

Day One (optional—to prepare ahead)

Mascarpone Cream: Place wine and shallots in small, heavy saucepan. Boil until almost dry, about 6 minutes. Add cream and boil until reduced by half, about 2 minutes. Stir in mascarpone, lemon peel, and chives. Cover and chill. Reheat when serving.

Cider Reduction: Place cider, vinegar and shallots in medium-size, heavy saucepan. Boil until reduced to ¾ cup, about 15 minutes. Strain, discard solids in strainer. Put cider reduction in container, cover, and refrigerate.

Day Two (Prepare on day you are serving)

Lentils: Press thin end of whole cloves into peeled onion. Place onion in heavy saucepan. Add water, lentils, and bay leaves. Bring to boil. Reduce heat to medium-low and simmer until lentils are tender, stirring occasionally, about 30 minutes.

Meanwhile, cook bacon in large, heavy skillet over medium heat until crisp. Using a slotted spoon, transfer to paper towels. Pour all but 3 tablespoons fat from skillet. Add shallots to skillet and sauté over medium heat until golden, about 2 minutes. Drain lentils, discarding onion and bay leaves. Add reserved bacon, lentils, and thyme to shallots.

Note: It is possible to make lentils 2 hours ahead. Let stand at room temperature and rewarm over medium heat, stirring often.

Scallops: Bring cider reduction to simmer. Whisk in 5 tablespoons butter, 1 tablespoon at a time. Keep warm. Season scallops with salt and pepper. Melt 1 tablespoon butter with oil in large, heavy skillet over medium-high heat. Add scallops and cook until brown, about 2 minutes per side.

To serve: Divide lentils among six plates. Arrange three scallops on top of lentils on each plate. Drizzle cider reduction over scallops and around lentils. Drizzle warm mascarpone cream over.

Homemade Ricotta Cheese
with Local Honeycomb and Grilled Bread

SERVES 6–8

Chef Snow serves this dish on a rectangular platter. The ricotta cheese is in a small canning jar with a piece of honeycomb and several pieces of grilled bread on the side. It is a very "homey" presentation for the dish's knockout taste.

Equipment: 6–8 canning jars (4–6 ounces) or small bowls

For the ricotta:

1 quart milk
1 quart heavy cream
3 tablespoons fresh lemon juice (or white vinegar)
1 tablespoon kosher salt
Honeycomb, small piece

For the grilled sourdough:

½ cup extra-virgin olive oil
4 tablespoons butter, melted
Pinch of salt and pepper
1 baguette sourdough bread, cut into ¼–½ inch slices

To prepare: Line a fine-mesh strainer with cheesecloth and set over a large bowl. Set aside. Place milk and cream in a large, heavy-bottomed saucepan. Bring to a boil over medium heat, stirring occasionally. Add lemon juice (or vinegar) and reduce heat. Simmer until mixture curdles, about 5–7 minutes. When separated, slowly drain through cheesecloth-covered strainer. After draining for 10 minutes, add salt and stir. Allow to drain for an additional 10 minutes. Discard extra liquid. Divide among canning jars or small bowls.

To prepare grilled sourdough: Mix oil with melted butter, salt and pepper. Brush slices of bread with oil mixture on each side. Grill until toasted on each side but soft in the center.

To serve: Serve immediately (or chill) with grilled sourdough bread and a piece of local honeycomb.

Pomegranate Custard

SERVES 6 (10 OUNCES EACH)

Equipment: 6 small (10-ounce) ramekins or oven-safe bowls

For the custard base:

1⅓ cups milk

5 cups heavy cream

12 egg yolks

¾ cup sugar

4 teaspoon vanilla

For the pomegranate curd:

12 eggs

2¼ cups sugar

2 cups pomegranate molasses

To prepare custard: Scald milk and cream in heavy-bottom saucepan. Whisk egg yolks with sugar and add vanilla. Strain, pour into a pitcher and skim bubbles off the custard. Place ramekins in baking pan and add water to halfway point on ramekins. From pitcher, pour custard into ramekins. Cover baking pan with foil and place in pre-heated 350°F oven for 45 minutes or until set (edges firm, but custard still jiggles in the center). Remove ramekins from water bath and cool on rack.

To prepare pomegranate curd: Whisk together eggs, sugar, and pomegranate molasses. Place in top of double boiler and simmer until it thickens. Be sure not to curdle (if it curdles, strain the liquid). Cool. Place pomegranate curd in pastry bag with small tip and apply to top of custard about ¼ inch thick.

Food Producers

Blue Hill Farm and Restaurant
The Meat Market

Blue Hill Farm Owners: Dan and David Barber;
Farm Manager: Sean Stanton;
The Meat Market Owner: Jeremy Stanton
Great Barrington

Two sets of brothers from the Berkshires, Dan and David Barber and Jeremy and Sean Stanton, are making a mark on the national food scene. Let's start with the Barber family.

Blue Hill Farm and Restaurant

Dan and David grew up on Blue Hill Farm. Their grandmother recorded an amusing tale of how the farm came to belong to the Barber family:

"I used to walk up Blue Hill Road every week, for years. . . . I loved Blue Hill Farm more than anything in the world. Back then it was a dairy run by two brothers. What a mess! They had cows pasturing in the front yard, for god's sake. . . . And the barn and house were run down and so dirty I couldn't believe it. And you know what? I loved it. I loved the open pastures, I loved the backdrop of blue hills, I loved that I felt like a queen every time I came up here. But whenever I told the brothers I wanted to buy the farm, they just laughed. 'Lady,' they'd say, 'this farm has been in our family for three generations. We're never selling.' I'd return the next week, and they'd say the same thing. 'Never selling.' This went on for years.

"Then one day I arrived at the top of the hill and one of the brothers came running over to me. 'Ma'am, do you still want to buy this farm?' I couldn't believe it. He didn't even let me answer. 'My brother and I have gotten into the biggest fight. If we don't sell it now we're going to kill each other.' I told them I was interested. 'Ma'am,' he said, 'we're selling it now, or forget it. Right now.' So I said yes. I hadn't even been inside the farmhouse, and I didn't know where the property began and where it ended. But it didn't matter. I just knew this was the place."

As young men, Dan and David made their way to New York City and opened a restaurant that they named after the family farm, Blue Hill. The Barber brothers hired their neighbor and friend, Sean Stanton, to manage the family farm and supply foods for the restaurant from the farm. The restaurant is extremely popular because customers recognize the fine quality of the foods sourced to the restaurants and cooked by the creative genius of Chef Dan Barber, while his brother David manages the business.

These two small-town Barber boys are now renowned. Dan, a true visionary, was named one of *Time* magazine's hundred most influential persons in 2009 for his research, contemplation, and writings about the future of sustainable food and agriculture. His new book *The Third Plate*, published in 2014, is creating quite a stir, since in it Dan pronounces that the farm-to-table movement isn't "working." He lays out the necessary steps of how we need to alter our nation's entire food system.

Dan and David are now the owners of another restaurant, Blue Hill at Stone Barns, located on the grounds of the Stone Barns Center for Food and Agriculture, a farm and educational center thirty miles from New York City. The spectacular stone barns have been part of the Rockefeller family's estates for three generations, and David Rockefeller and his daughter Peggy Dulany helped found this four-season farm and educational institution. One of Stone Barns' most significant annual events is the Young Farmers Conference, the only conference of its size and scope with a mission to educate new farmers about issues and skills they will need to survive. There are no menus at Blue Hill at Stone Barns. Instead, guests are offered the multi-taste "Grazing, Pecking, Rooting" menu featuring the best offerings from the field and market.

Meanwhile, back in Great Barrington, let's pick up the thread to the Stanton brothers—Sean, the manager of Blue Hill Farm, and his brother, Jeremy Stanton, proprietor of The Meat Market.

Sean has revitalized the Blue Hill Farm pastures with an intensive rotation plan and by adding extra lime to the fields. At first, with barren fields and tasteless grass, Sean had difficulty getting the cows to graze, and their milk was inferior. Now the fields are lush and rich with minerals and vitamins.

Sean's cows produce high-quality milk with a five-star rating. Sean is experimenting with a new approach—allowing the calf to stay with the mother for a while after birth. Most dairy farms want to sell the milk from the lactating cow's milk immediately, and the calf is weaned away quickly. The separation is traumatic for the mother and calf, but the goal is to maximize the volume of the salable milk for the farmer. Farmers like Sean and Topher Sabot of Cricket Creek Farm are taking note of recent evidence indicating that the mother and calf both benefit from delaying the weaning process Besides gaining antibodies from nursing, the calves grow faster, and the calf becomes a better mother when she has her own calves.

It was milk that got Sean involved with farming. After service in the US Coast Guard, Sean returned to Great Barrington to his family farm, North Plains Farm, to attend college. Sean grew up on the family farm, which housed some special-needs individuals. Sean's parents were proponents of the Rudolf Steiner philosophy and Camphill communities, which provide opportunities for mentally disabled people to live with others and share in the daily life and tasks of the house and land.

Sean says, "It was good to be home where I had access to buying fresh, raw milk, which I loved since I had grown up drinking it. But I had a voracious appetite and soon I owed $160 to Moon in the Pond Farm, the supplier of my raw milk." Farmer Dominic Palumbo, a local committed farmer in the region, suggested Sean work off his debt. While working on the Moon in the Pond

Farm, Sean started down the path to becoming a farmer himself. Sean looks back and is glad he became a self-educated farmer. He feels it has allowed him to be more open to new ideas, rather than rejecting opportunities because "it isn't the way farming is done." Sean read books, researched the Internet, attended workshops, asked farmers to mentor him, and networked with many of the great farmers and food producers who are part of the vibrant Berkshire Grown nonprofit.

To farm, Sean needed land but, like many young farmers, he didn't have the money to buy land. Instead Sean leased land from as many as twelve different properties. He raised cows, pigs, and hens. A couple of years into his farmer life, he met Dan Barber, the local boy made famous as the chef of Blue Hill Restaurant. Dan asked Sean to manage the family farm and, a year and a half later, Sean decided to accept. Sean manages and works Blue Hill Farm with the help of two full-time apprentices and apprentices who come for the summer. Sean is a knowledgeable farmer. He is always experimenting in order to find new ways of raising animals to be healthy, tasty, and sustainable. His cows feed 100 percent on grass and hay raised on his farm. Now Sean wants to feed the pigs and chickens with homegrown grains and forage. Recently Sean has embarked on a side venture. He is raising cows at North Main Farm, where the milk is used to make savory flavored yogurts for Blue Hill Restaurant at Stone Barns. The cows and pigs that Sean raises at North Main Farm are sold to his brother's new store and cafe, The Meat Market.

Sean is providing many of the meats and all of the tomatoes he can raise for one of the most prominent restaurants in New York City and in America, Blue Hill Restaurant, headed by a revolutionary thinker and chef, Dan Barber. Not bad for a young guy.

The Meat Market

The Meat Market was established by Sean's brother, Jeremy. When Jeremy decided to set up a butcher shop and cafe, there were lots of doubters. Thus it was with an adventurous spirit and expertise in the butchering and curing of meats that Jeremy opened his store, The Meat Market. The market offers quality (and custom) cuts of meat and a line of artisanal charcuterie, porchetta, salami, and guanciale to fulfill the purpose of a "nose to tail" butcher shop. Jeremy's limits his animal sources to a few select farms where he knows how the animals are raised. Every cut of meat at The Meat Market reflects the Berkshire microclimate, the soil, and the animal. You would think you had arrived in a European butcher shop when you survey the range of prepared meats, including pâté, fresh sausages, bacon, rillettes, coppa, pancetta, guanciale, and a variety of dry-cured sausages, plus more unusual

charcuterie items like shacon (mutton bacon), New Lebanon baloney, and *testa in cassetta*. Amid the hanging sausages in the center of the store is the centerpiece: large butcher blocks where one or two butchers are busy preparing custom cuts of meat.

The Meat Market offers quality meats and prepared foods, a sit-down cafe, space for classes (such as sausage making), and special events like its annual spring lamb roast. There is a mix of fun and reverence for food going on at this unique store. Jeremy comments, "We here at The Meat Market are honored to be part of this avant-garde food culture (which looks remarkably like the pre–World War II food culture): good food made in local soil by neighbors and friends, food fed by the earth that feeds us—no middle men required."

Jeremy had already established a successful catering business, Fire Roasted Catering, focused on the theme of roasting whole animals outdoors on spits. In partnership with a welder, Jeremy designed many of the roasting devices, such as a vertical stand with a fire in the center, and a turning circle of chickens, ducks, turkeys, or lambs hung from metal chains, which rotate and turn as they cook. One piece of equipment is large enough to roast a thousand-pound cow.

Fire Roasted Catering creates memorable events at venues all over the northeast: the meats crackling and roasting, wooden tables groaning with food and drink, and Jeremy working the scene in his fire-resistant leather chaps. Maybe it is the cowboy atmosphere or Jeremy's charisma, but these meat-roasting catered parties are truly once-in-a-lifetime experiences. Yet, Jeremy regretted that his services of outdoor roasting or grilling of meats, making sausages, and preparing charcuterie were often away from his hometown. Figuring out how to bring meat to the Berkshires led to his opening The Meat Market, with his veterinarian wife, Emily. The former editor-in-chief of *Gourmet* magazine, Ruth Reichl, a regional summer resident and big supporter of Jeremy's, was one of his first investors.

By the time I visited, the market was in full swing with butchers cutting, customers chatting and buying meat, and people dining. There wasn't a plastic-wrapped Styrofoam tray of meat in sight. Instead, there are hanging artisanal sausages. When I asked Jeremy about one sausage, he launched into an utterly fascinating story about Spanish conquerers who left Iberian pigs on Ossabaw Island in Georgia during the sixteenth century. Then there's a subplot involving a Native American princess, but let's skip over a few centuries to modern times, when this breed of pig was almost eliminated by Georgia's Department of Natural Resources. They had discovered the island pig carried a disease that could infect mainland pigs, and hunters were allowed to come to the island and shoot the pigs.

Fortunately, a few were saved. Now endangered, some Ossabaw pigs are being raised at select facilities at a few universities and at some farms in the Berkshires. Jeremy purchases their meat and converts it into extraordinary sausages. (At some of the universities raising the Ossabaw pig, researchers are testing the pigs for their "thrifty gene," which may unlock some of the clues to diabetes.) Jeremy says the Ossabaw is a cute pig with a long nose, evolved for foraging, and dainty feet. You never know what you are going to learn in a butcher shop.

It's extraordinary that the small town of Great Barrington, Massachusetts, has produced two sets of brothers—four individuals—who are making such significant contributions to how food is raised, prepared, and offered to the public. Their leadership is changing and influencing the world.

Farm Recipes

Grilled Tuna Steaks with Ginger

SERVES 4

Old Friends Farm, Home of Northeast Grown Ginger, Amherst
Owners: Casey Steinberg and Missy Bahret

I encourage you to buy tender, young ginger. Though more perishable than the older, brown-colored ginger, the young ginger freezes well. If you visit the farm to buy ginger, you'll enjoy purchasing many other vegetables and spectacular cut flowers. You almost want to have a party as an excuse to fill a space with their flowers and produce.

1 cup bottled teriyaki sauce (or make your own—see note below)
½ teaspoon fresh ginger, peeled and minced
½ teaspoon garlic, minced
4 tuna steaks, about 2 pounds

To marinate tuna: Mix teriyaki sauce, ginger, and garlic in a shallow dish. Marinate tuna steaks in refrigerator for at least 1 hour, turning 2–3 times.

Grill the tuna: Preheat the grill. Place the steaks on grill and cook until done, about 3 minutes on each side, depending on thickness of tuna.

To make your own teriyaki sauce: ⅛ cup tamari, ½ cup water, ¼ teaspoon ginger powder, 2 tablespoons brown sugar, 1 tablespoon honey. Heat until sugar dissolves. Mix 1 tablespoon cornstarch with ⅛ cup water and stir into sauce. Heat until sauce thickens.

Spicy Yogurt Dressing

Swartz Family Farm, Amherst
Owners: Joe and Sarah Swartz

Four generations of the Swartz family have been part of the history of the Pioneer Valley. Brothers John and Anastazi Swartz emigrated from Poland in 1919 and, after working on other farms, were able to buy forty acres. John's two sons took over the farms and diversified, particularly through their decision to substitute other crops for tobacco, which was fast declining as a good revenue source. When John's son Joe inherited the farm, he felt it would be best to focus on one intensive crop, so he transformed the business into a large-scale hydroponic lettuce and vegetable farm. Joe and Sarah continue to operate Swartz Farm today.

1 cup plain yogurt
1½ tablespoons confectioners' sugar
¼ teaspoon cinnamon
½ teaspoon cardamom
⅛ teaspoon nutmeg
1 tablespoon finely chopped mint leaves

To prepare: Place the yogurt in a bowl and beat in the sugar and spices until well blended. Fold in the mint and chill. Excellent served with all fruits, over a fruit salad, or as dressing for lettuce salad.

Rhubarb Streusel Coffee Cake

SERVES 8

Moon in the Pond Farm, Sheffield
Owner: Dominic Palumbo

Moon in the Pond Farm is mentioned in the profile of Sean Stanton, farmer for Blue Hill Restaurant, as the place where Sean was first inspired to take farming seriously. No wonder. Farmer Dominic Palumbo is a teacher and mentor who has influenced farmers and farming in the Berkshires and beyond. Moon in the Pond is exclusively dedicated to heritage breed animals and heirloom vegetables, and Dominic combines traditional farming methods (oxen to plow) with modern technology. Moon in the Pond was organic before most people knew what the term meant. Farmer Dom says he wants to deliver "the best, cleanest, most wholesome, nutritious, exquisitely delicious food." Try his recipe for spring rhubarb.

Equipment: 9 x 13-inch baking pan, lightly greased and floured

For the cake:

1 ¼ cups milk

1 tablespoon white distilled or cider vinegar

2 ¼ cups unbleached all-purpose flour

1 teaspoon baking soda

½ teaspoon sea salt

8 tablespoons (1 stick) butter, unsalted

1 ½ cups brown sugar, light or dark

1 large egg

3 cups rhubarb, sliced ½-inch thick

For the topping:

½ cup brown sugar, light or dark

½ rolled oats, old fashioned, not instant

1 ½ teaspoons ground cinnamon

To prepare: Combine milk and vinegar and let stand until the milk curdles, about 5 minutes. Mix the flour, baking soda, and salt in a large bowl. Cream the butter and brown sugar together with an electric beater on high speed until the mixture is light and fluffy, about 3 minutes. Beat in the egg. Then in three stages, starting with the flour, stir in alternating portions of the flour and curdled milk. Lightly mix till barely blended; do not overmix. Fold in the rhubarb. Spread the batter evenly in the cake pan.

To prepare the topping: Mix sugar, oats, and cinnamon in small bowl with your fingers or fork until mixed thoroughly. Sprinkle over the batter.

To bake: Place pan in 350°F preheated oven and bake for 35–40 minutes, or until a knife inserted in the center of the cake comes out clean. Cool on cake rack.

Is spring ever so overwhelmingly beautiful that you almost want to cry at the new life miraculously appearing? The Pioneer Valley and Berkshires are lime green in the spring. Ramps and fiddlehead ferns and asparagus are special delicacies of the season and available to forage or eat—sumptuously prepared—in any number of restaurants.

Williamsville Inn and Mushroom Foraging, West Stockbridge

German-born Erhard Wendt, the co-owner of the Williamsville Inn, grew up eating and foraging mushrooms. He uses mushrooms in many of the dishes served in the inn's dining room. When guests raved over his mushrooms, Erhard began to offer seminars about mushrooms, including afternoon foraging trips. The inn is a historic eighteenth-century inn with ten acres of organic gardens, plus tennis courts, swimming pools, and fine dining. Contact Erhard through the inn or another local mushroom and edible plants expert, Russ Cohen, who has written a book on foraging and guides foraging trips in the Berkshires. http://users.rcn.com/eatwild/bio.htm

Pekarski's Sausage, South Deerfield

In the winter you might have stopped at Pekarski's store to buy andouille sausage, but now that it is spring, buy a smoked ham or Cornish hen. Mike Pekarski is the third generation operating an artisanal smokehouse where he makes six to eight hundred pounds of kielbasa per week during nonholiday times, but in preparation for the holidays like Easter, Pekarski does that quantity in a single day. For the traditional Easter meal, Mike—and his extended family, including three aunts who work in the family business—smoke over five hundred hams. Their meats are prepared in three smokers burning local hardwoods like apple, cherry, hickory, and maple. Besides smoking ham and several types of sausage including Polish kielbasa, Pekarski sells excellent bacon and breakfast links, turkeys, chicken, and Cornish game hens. It's a simple, single-food store where you can buy meat for a snack or picnic or to take home.

Atkins Farms, Amherst

If you don't have time to visit local farms individually, you can get almost anything you want at the Atkins Farms store. They sell their spring fruits—strawberries and lots of vegetables, plus they stock produce from many of the local farms, like Mapleline Farm, milk in glass bottles, some of the limited production of Snow's ice cream, and Atkins' famous cider doughnuts.

Gould's Sugar House, Shelburne Falls

This is an old favorite venue for families who have been coming here for generations to be greeted by Mrs. Gould. The restaurant opens March 1, and as an homage to spring and the running of the maple tree sap that is turned into syrup, try your first ice cream of the season—Gould's maple-flavored soft-serve. Most people come for the blueberry pancakes, corn fritters, and homemade sausages, all of which should be eaten with Gould's maple syrup. The most fun is watching the syrup-making operation on the lower level of the restaurant. You can buy a bottle of still-hot syrup to take home.

The Meat Market, Great Barrington

Visit this specialty meat store and cafe where Jeremy Stanton butchers and sells local grass-fed, pastured meats from a few selected vendors including his brother Sean, who is the farmer supplying meats to the Blue Hill restaurants in New York and at Stone Barns. Read more about The Meat Market earlier in this section.

Moon in the Pond, Sheffield

Farmer Dominic Palumbo is as much a teacher as a farmer. He loves to share and exchange knowledge of biodynamic farming, combining traditional methods with best contemporary practices. The heritage breeds are fascinating to observe. Moon in the Pond is a nonprofit farm that donates 1 percent of any profits to 1% for the Planet, an organization with members in forty-eight countries. The farm holds small educational workshops and programs. The farm is open seven days a week during daylight hours. E-mail Dom@mooninthepond.org if you wish to visit the farm or sign up for any of the educational offerings. Buy farm produce on Wednesday and Friday at Rubiners' Cheesemonger on Main Street, Great Barrington. Look for the charcuterie!

Farm Girl Farm, Sheffield

Another great farm in Sheffield. Order ahead (laura@farmgirlfarm.com) and drive to 1237 Bow Wow Lane on Memorial Day weekend to pick up flats of seedlings of vegetable and herbs. Healthy plants at a great price.

Nudel, Lenox

You can tell this place is cool by its slightly eccentric logo. The restaurant's slogan, "seasonally inspired food," is a true statement. The food is truly inspired. Ingredients are mixed in new ways with delicious outcomes. The restaurant mission is a commitment to "local, organic, ethical, and natural." This is a relatively new twenty-seven-seat restaurant, opened by a chef, Bjorn Somlo, who grew up in the Berkshires. Dinner only. Closed Sunday. No reservations.

Upinngil Farm, Gill

A father-daughter operation situated on a lovely farm, which looks out from a high point to rolling hills with Ayrshire English grazing cows. The gentle, sweet landscape might give you the impression that life is slow at this farm, but dad Cliff Hatch and daughter Sorrell Hatch are two busy people. The farm grows organic wheat, rye, and buckwheat that Sorrel transforms into all sorts of delicious baked goods and pies, many of which she sells at her Little Red Hen Bakery. Freshly milled flour is also for sale. Cliff tends the cows and grows grain and grapes—many of which are made into wine. The cows' glass-bottled raw milk is available, as are farm cheeses. Cliff offers cheesemaking workshops, and the store carries equipment and cultures for home dairy craft, including yogurt- and cheesemaking.

Moon & Dove, Amherst

A beer pub with lots of beer on tap and a huge stock of bottled beer from all over the world. The only reason a place like this—which doesn't serve food—can stay in business is due to its excellent focus on beer. It is possible to order food to be delivered here and there are free peanuts.

Mezze Bar and Grill, Williamstown

This restaurant bar and grill overlooking Sheep Hill is extremely well regarded for its support of local farmers and food producers. The menu changes weekly, even daily, depending on the availability of the freshest ingredients. The menu is paired with suggestions from local microbreweries and distilleries. The Mezze Group, which owns and operates this restaurant, manages another restaurant, Allium, in Great Barrington.

SPRING TOUR

Peace Valley Farm and Williams College, Williamstown

Near Mezze Bar and Grill in Williamstown is Williams College, where there are lots of cultural offerings, including a highly ranked Williams College Theater Festival in July and August and the Clark Art Institute. Williams College has a close working relationship with Peace Valley Farm, which provides many of the vegetables for the college kitchen facility. As part of their partnership, Peace Valley Farm accepts Williams College student interns to work summers on the farm. If you call ahead (413-458-4866), the farm can usually accommodate visitors. If they are too busy, you can always take a self-guided tour.

Summer

Small Plate

Tea Eggs Two Ways

It seems everyone is keeping backyard chickens these days. One of the things I love about having my own chickens is the variety of egg sizes produced by my different chicken breeds. If you aren't raising your own chickens, you'll find organic, free-range chickens in every farmers' market. You'll notice the different size eggs (unless the farmer only raises one breed of chicken).

"Little plates" and appetizers are always challenging for me. Give me main courses or desserts! So, tea eggs are often my "go-to nibble" thanks to the years I spent living and traveling in Asia. They are pretty, full of protein, and not fattening. The recipe only makes four eggs, so you might want to multiply it to suit your own purposes. I am including a second, non-Asian method for making tea eggs, a version taught to me by a Russian ballet dancer. It involves a bit more work (wrapping the eggs) but is a terrific project to do with children because when unwrapping the eggs, every egg design is different with surprising marbleized results.

Tea Eggs #1

SERVES 4

4 eggs
4 cups water
2–3 tea bags, or 2–3 teaspoons loose black tea
1 tablespoon soy sauce
1 tablespoon salt
2 star anise
1 stick cinnamon
1 piece ginger, sliced into pieces (optional)
Zest of orange or lemon

To prepare: Cover eggs with water, bring water to simmer, turn off heat, and simmer for 15 minutes. Transfer to cold water, retaining pan of hot water. Gently crack eggshell with back of spoon to create small patterns. Place eggs in hot water with tea, soy sauce, salt, anise, cinnamon, ginger, and orange or lemon zest and simmer for 1 hour or longer. Refrigerate overnight or longer. Eggs will keep unpeeled for several days. Peel eggs when you are ready to serve them and watch the tiny veins of brown emerge.

To serve: Serve whole for dipping in Szechuan pepper (recipe follows) or slice and sprinkle salt over eggs.

Tea Eggs #2

SERVES 4

Dry, loose skins of red or brown onions, enough to cover
    4 eggs
Small scraps of thin cloth, 3 x 4 inches
4 eggs
Twine
2–3 bags black tea, or 2–3 teaspoons loose tea
3 tablespoons vinegar
Homemade mayonnaise (optional)

Szechuan pepper:
3 tablespoons Szechuan peppercorns
2 teaspoons coriander seeds
1 tablespoon Chinese 5-spice powder
2 tablespoons salt

To prepare: Place onion skins on fabric, each egg on top of skins in center and wrap cloth around egg. Tie ends of cloth with twine, securing cloth as tightly against the egg as possible (the more pressure on the onion skin, the prettier the design) without cracking the egg. Place eggs in saucepan, cover with water, add tea and vinegar and simmer for 20 minutes. Cool and take off fabric. The eggs will be covered with brown/reddish veins from the onion peel.

To prepare Szechuan pepper: Roast peppercorns and coriander seeds in a dry, hot, heavy-bottom cast-iron skillet or similar pan. Toast for 3 minutes. Do not burn. Stir in 5-spice powder and salt. Let cool. With mortar and pestle or electric spice mill, grind spices. Store in container with a tight-sealing lid.

To serve: Serve with eggshells on and allow guests to peel the eggs. Dip in Szechuan pepper or homemade mayonnaise.

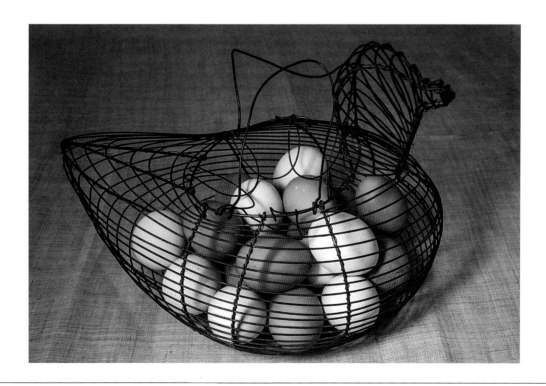

Brunch

Asparagus with Shaker Lemon Sauce

SERVES 4

My mother had this recipe in her recipe box on one of those 3 x 5 file cards. I don't know if the sauce has a legitimate connection to the Shakers, the religious sect of visionary, sustainable farming, but it is a delicious sauce.

Fresh asparagus is an extraordinary vegetable. In places like Alsace, France, the restaurants advertise their asparagus specials when asparagus is in season. Dutch friends of mine were so excited to see asparagus in the Paris markets that they bought a couple of pounds to take home to their families. Francesca, my Italian friend, and I went to the market to buy asparagus and debated all the way home as to how to best prepare them. I didn't have this recipe with me at the time, but I have since sent it to Francesca, so the Shaker influence has now reached Italy.

1 pound asparagus

1 cup light cream

2 tablespoons butter

1 teaspoon finely minced mint

¼ teaspoon salt

1 egg yolk, beaten

1 teaspoon lemon juice

½ teaspoon freshly grated nutmeg

To prepare the asparagus: Snap the fibrous ends off the asparagus. The asparagus will snap at just the right point when you bend the spear. If you want to be fancy, you can use a vegetable peeler to remove some of the points and outer skin of the asparagus. For a small amount of asparagus, lay them flat in a frying pan with a thin layer of water. Boil water with lid on pan, and the asparagus will be cooked in just a few minutes. For a large amount of asparagus, tie the bunch (or bunches) together and place in 2 inches of boiling water. Cover and steam for 4–6 minutes till asparagus are ready. Asparagus should be tender enough to be pierced with a fork, but not be overcooked and mushy.

To make sauce: Combine cream, butter, mint, and salt in a saucepan. Bring to boil and boil for 5 minutes till cream is reduced to ¾ cup. In the dish with your egg yolk, stir in 2 tablespoons of the warm cream mixture from your saucepan. Stirring constantly, pour egg yolk mixture into the cream mixture in the saucepan. Do not allow to boil. Stir in lemon juice.

To serve: Lay asparagus in an oval serving dish. Pour sauce in a wide band across the middle of the asparagus and grate some nutmeg over sauce.

Bread

Ann Van Stelten's Oatmeal Bread

APPROXIMATELY 10 SLICES

Long before Jim Leahy's overnight, no-knead bread with its long fermentation time (to create a sourdough flavor) and high hydration (to cause the grains to release more nutrients), was the huge rage, as popularized by Mark Bittman's column in the *New York Times*, my mother was using the same formula for bread she baked for our family. Today my brother and I bake this bread, especially at Thanksgiving, as a way to celebrate my mother's legacy. The bread makes great sandwiches, but I like the bread toasted.

1 tablespoon dry instant yeast
2¼ cups water
8 cups flour
1 tablespoon salt
1 tablespoon butter
½ cup molasses, light or regular, not dark
1 heaping cup regular oat flakes, not instant

To prepare yeast: Mix yeast with ¼ cup warm tap water. Stir to mix.

To make dough: Place flour, salt, butter, molasses, and oats in large mixing bowl or pan. Add 2 cups hot tap water. Stir. When the mixture is cool, add the yeast and mix well.

To ferment: Cover with damp towel and leave at room temperature for 12–16 hours, or overnight.

Next day: Divide the dough into two, shape into loaves and place in greased loaf pans. Let rise till double in size, probably 2–3 hours, depending on temperature of the kitchen.

To bake: Bake at 350°F for 75 minutes until the tops are a caramel color. Remove loaves from pans and let cool completely on a wire rack before cutting.

Soups

Pappa al Pomodoro
(Tomato and Bread Soup)

SERVES 4–6

This soup is thick and homey and a meal unto itself. Francesca Barbini, my dear Italian friend, lives an elegant life in Venice, but she also appreciates the robust flavors of country cooking. She shared this recipe with me. I often can tomatoes at the end of the summer especially to have some tomatoes in the fall and winter for this recipe. Francesca insists that skins should be removed from the tomatoes. Basil is a key ingredient. Remember, basil should be torn and not chopped. Supposedly a metal knife reduces the flavor. Fortunately, big chunks of basil are great in this soup. Tomatoes and basil are abundant in the Berkshires and Pioneer Valley. Please enjoy this soup.

6 pounds large, ripe tomatoes (bruised or seconds are fine, but buy a few more if you are going to lose some parts of the tomato)

1 cup olive oil

5 cloves garlic, peeled and chopped

1 bunch basil, leaves pulled off stems (tear up larger leaves and use small leaves intact)

2 pounds of 1- or 2-day-old country-style artisanal bread, with lots of air pockets and good crumb

3–5 cups water as needed

1 teaspoon salt

1 teaspoon pepper

For the garnish:

Few basil leaves

Grated Parmesan cheese

To prepare tomatoes: Boil large kettle of water. Cut small cross incision on bottom of tomatoes and drop each in the boiling water. Remove the tomatoes from water with slotted spoon or some type of strainer. Peel skins off tomatoes and squeeze out some or all of seeds.

To prepare the soup: Heat ½ cup olive oil in large, heavy-bottom skillet over medium heat. Add garlic and sauté till soft. Add tomatoes and basil. Reduce heat to medium and simmer for 30 minutes. Tear bread into chunks and put into tomato mixture. Add water to cover tomato-bread mixture. Add salt, pepper, and remaining ½ cup olive oil. Simmer till bread and tomatoes fall apart. The texture of the soup should be thick.

To serve: Serve with a few basil leaves as decoration and grate a little Parmesan cheese over soup.

Blueberry Gazpacho

SERVES 4

Blueberries are a little jewel of a fruit. Tart, with a familiar taste, blueberries say "home" to many people who live in the Berkshires or Pioneer Valley. Visitors eagerly look forward to muffins or pancakes with fresh, not frozen blueberries. One unusual way to use blueberries is in the traditional Spanish soup gazpacho. You will be totally refreshed if you have this soup on a hot summer's day.

1 pound dark purple seedless grapes

½ cup grape juice, or blueberry or lingonberry concentrate from Ikea (½ cup concentrate plus ¼ cup water)

2 tablespoons honey

12 ounces fresh blueberries

2 medium tomatoes

1 red pepper

1 green pepper

1 medium onion

2 cloves garlic, minced

1 seedless cucumber, chopped

¼ teaspoon salt

2 tablespoons lemon juice

1 cup Greek-style yogurt

2 small mint leaves for each serving of soup

To prepare: Remove grapes from stems and place in 4-quart saucepan. Add grape juice and honey and bring to boil. Reduce and simmer for 15 minutes. Let cool and then put grape juice and blueberries in food processor. Pulse and add juice.

Meanwhile, chop tomatoes, peppers, and onion into cubes and add to grape-blueberry mixture. Add garlic and cucumbers. Adjust flavor by adding honey, salt, and lemon. If soup is too thick, thin a bit with more juice or water. Chill thoroughly, several hours but preferably overnight.

To serve: Garnish with Greek-style yogurt and few leaves of mint.

Salads

Diet Asian Salad
with Chopped Peanuts and Dressing

SERVES 8

I call this my "diet" salad. My son calls it my "rabbit" food. I got hooked on it nearly two years ago and still frequently have it for lunch. I make a "bucket" of the sliced cabbage, grated carrot, and herbs. In two other containers, I store the chopped peanuts and dressing. I can quickly assemble the salad—chopping up an apple, adding the pre-cut cabbage, carrot, and herb mixture, perhaps throwing in some leftovers and then mixing in the salad dressing and topping it off with chopped nuts. It's really addictive!

I gained some weight writing my book on bread baking and, without dieting, just by eating this salad for lunch, I lost ten pounds. This cold salad is perfect on a hot day.

For the salad:

12 cups green or purple cabbage

2 carrots, grated through large or hand-held grater

½ bunch cilantro, washed and coarsely chopped

3 apples, cut in half and then chopped coarsely

For the dressing:

6 tablespoons soy sauce

4 teaspoons brown sugar

4 tsp nuoc mam (Vietnamese or Thai fish sauce)

2 limes, juice and zest

1 jalapeño pepper

8 tablespoons peanut oil

For the topping:

Peanuts, roasted, unsalted, chopped fairly fine

To prepare salad: Cut cabbage finely with mandoline grater. Grate carrots and add to cabbage. Then add cilantro. Salad can be stored in refrigerator at this point. Cut and add apples just before serving; this will prevent them from turning brown and mushy in the refrigerator.

To make dressing: Add all ingredients together. Place in jar with lid, close, and shake.

To serve: Place cabbage salad mixture in a single serving bowl, add apple. Toss with dressing and garnish with lots of peanuts.

Niçoise Salad

SERVES 4

Though this is a recipe from southern France, it is perfect for the Berkshires and Pioneer Valley since the salad is composed of vegetables that are abundant at farmers' markets in the summer. There is something great about the combination of flavors, plus the fun of cutting up the different ingredients and deciding which two (or three) to put on the fork for each bite. I am a fan of recipes that can be made ahead of time, which gives me time with my guests. Even though I have assembled this salad many times, I am writing it down for the first time.

Since the colors and textures are a key part of the presentation, it is important to decoratively lay out each plate, with the tuna fish as the hub of the wheel and the vegetables like spokes. To be sure your hard-boiled egg doesn't have a gray, greenish ring between the white and yolk, follow directions below for hard-boiling an egg. Cover salad with plastic wrap and place in refrigerator until ready to serve.

4 beets, small to medium red (or even various colors)

12 small potatoes (red skin, fingerling, or Yukon Gold)

2 pounds green beans

1½ pounds asparagus

4 eggs

1–2 heads lettuce, preferably Boston

2 cans tuna, solid white

2 bell peppers, red, yellow, or green

4 ripe tomatoes, medium size, cut into 8 slices

For the garnish:

Capers and cornichons

To cook vegetables: Cover beets with water, bring to boil, and then simmer for approximately 20–30 minutes until a knife can pierce through the center easily. While beets are still warm, peel off skins. In separate pan, cook potatoes about 5 minutes, until a knife can pierce through the center. Steam green beans and asparagus till al dente.

To boil the egg: Place eggs in pan. Cover with 1 inch of cold water and bring water to boil. Take off the heat, cover pan, and let eggs sit for 12 minutes. Drain water and peel eggs while still warm. They will be easier to peel.

To begin salad preparation: Place clean lettuce leaves on each of the four plates. Press down to create flat surface. Divide tuna fish among four plates and place in center. Cut the eggs in half and place two halves on each plate at 12 and 6 o'clock. Cut the peppers and remove stems and seeds and slice in strips about ½-inch wide. Arrange on salad in two separate locations opposite each other.

To arrange the beans and asparagus: Divide the beans and asparagus into eight portions. Arrange two portions of beans and asparagus on each plate at equal distances apart, such as beans at 1:30 and 7:30 o'clock and asparagus at 10:30 and 4:30.

To finish: Cut beets and potatoes in thin slices. Place in rows on the salad, opposite each other. Cut tomato in half and each half in four slices. Place on salad in appropriate locations, balancing the red/yellow of the pepper.

To garnish: Scatter cornichons and capers.

To serve: Pass salad dressing in pitcher for guests to add individually.

Entrees

Chicken with Apricots

SERVES 6

Head over to Clarkdale Fruit Farm or shop at most farmers' markets in July and nab those delectable little golden orange balls called apricots. I use apricots for pastry fillings and I love to make apricot jam, so I was a bit astonished when my friend Brenda used apricots in this main course dish. Brenda cooked her chicken with apricots for a meal when a group of friends was visiting me on Cranberry Island, Maine. I think everyone raved over the dish because not only was it delicious, but because apricots and chicken are an unusually satisfying combination.

Equipment: 9 x 13-inch baking pan

3 chicken breasts, boneless
3 yellow onions, peeled and diced
2 garlic cloves, minced
2 tablespoons olive oil
3 chicken bouillon cubes, low sodium
1 cup white wine
Water as needed
1½ cup rice, variety of your choice
½ cup celery
½ cup green and/or red bell pepper
½ teaspoon each of 3 of the following 5 herbs: basil,
    tarragon, rosemary, celery seed, coriander
5 ripe apricots (or dried apricots reconstituted in water)
Salt and pepper
½ cup grated soft cheese

For the garnish:
2 tablespoons parsley, chopped fine

To prepare chicken: Wash chicken and remove any bits of fat or cartilage. Using one hand to firmly hold chicken breast flat, slice each breast in two pieces horizontally to make 12 pieces of breast meat to roll around filling. Pound any thicker pieces to make all the pieces fairly similar.

To prepare filling: Slowly, over medium heat, sauté two onions and garlic in olive oil in saucepan until onions are very soft and slightly browned. Add chicken broth concentrate cubes, turn heat to low, mash the concentrate with a wooden spoon into the onions and keep stirring. Add ½ cup wine and some water if necessary. At this point the onion component will seem too strong in flavor, but keep in mind that this mixture will be dispersed through all of your chicken breasts and their filling, so being a little too strong at this point is OK. Reduce sauce till it is slightly thick.

Meanwhile: Prepare rice. Sauté remaining onion, celery, and pepper. Add herbs and taste. When rice is cooked, mix in the vegetables. Simmer chopped apricots in remaining ½ cup wine (or water) on very low heat until very soft.

To assemble: Spread half of the onion mixture in the bottom of the baking pan, along with the apricots. Put some rice filling in the center of each chicken piece, roll up and place in pan. Place the chicken rolls close together to prevent them from unrolling, or secure with string or toothpicks. Salt and pepper and the chicken rolls and cover with the remaining onion mixture.

To bake: Bake at 350°F in a preheated oven for 30 minutes. Sprinkle cheese over chicken and bake 15 more minutes. If you don't want the cheese to be soft and gooey, you can add the cheese when you first put the chicken in the oven and it will be crusty when finished. Garnish with parsley.

Wholesome Rice Salad

SERVES 8

I had my first rice salad on a French picnic in southern France forty years ago and have liked rice salads very much since. I created this rice recipe with mushrooms and raisins to add "interest" to the wholesome brown rice and amaranth (another ancient grain!). The recipe makes enough for two days and the joy of a rice—rather than a lettuce—salad is that it is good the next day. Enjoy and feel healthy with every bite.

3 cups oyster mushrooms (or any other type), torn or chopped into medium size pieces
3 cups coarsely chopped leeks
2 celery stalks, chopped
2 cloves garlic, peeled and minced
¼ cup olive oil
1¾ cup basmati rice, preferably brown
¼ cup wild rice
¼ cup amaranth
1 tablespoon soy sauce
2 teaspoons powdered chile pepper
1 teaspoon dried marjoram
1 teaspoon fresh mint, chopped finely

Additions (optional—use any or all):
¾ cup currants or golden raisins
2 tomatoes cut into chunks
1 cup black or small red beans, cooked or from can
1 cup cooked corn

To prepare grains: Sauté mushrooms, leeks, celery, and garlic in olive oil for about 10 minutes. Combine with grains, soy sauce, and spices with 4 cups water.

To bake: Place in 8-cup baking container and bake for 1½ hours at 375°F.

To make the salad: Let grains cool. Toss with fork and add optional raisins, cut tomatoes, beans, and corn if desired.

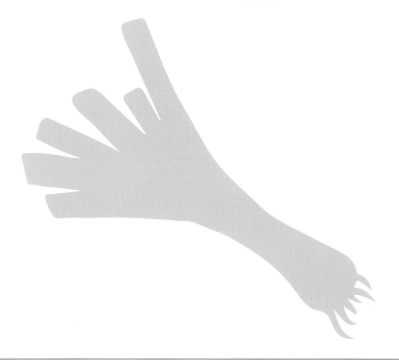

Pork with Spicy Chocolate Mole

SERVES 4

Moles are complex, and I have tried tasting and making many of them, especially since my daughter and I have been making annual trips to Mexico for nearly a decade. The following mole recipe has plenty of complexity but is also easy to make. Try it with the excellent free-range, no-hormone pork from pigs raised in the Berkshires and Pioneer Valley. Stories abound to explain how chocolate was introduced to this Mexican dish, but no matter its origin, the hint of chocolate—with the chile flavors—is really divine.

Equipment: Crock pot or dutch oven

1½–2 pounds pork shoulder, cut into cubes

For the sauce:
5 ancho chiles, rehydrated (save 1 cup water)

Note: guajillo, chile colorado, and pastilla chiles are also options. Buy in dry form at Hispanic food stores or any good supermarket.

1 onion, chopped
1 cloves garlic
1 tomato, quartered
1 cup whole raw almonds with skins
½ cup raisins
½ cup pumpkin seeds, raw or roasted, unsalted

¼ teaspoon each ground clove, cumin, and coriander, fresh or dried oregano, ground anise
1 teaspoon salt
1 cup water from rehydrating chiles
1–2 ounces dark unsweetened chocolate
¼ cup toasted sesame seeds

To prepare chiles: Remove stems from chiles and cover with hot water. Let soak till chiles soften. Drain and save 1 cup of liquid. (I suggest using the whole chiles and seeds. The mole won't be too hot, but if you are worried, you can discard the chile seeds.)

To make sauce: Preheat a large skillet over medium heat. Place the onion and garlic in the dry pan to toast on all sides. Put the tomatoes into the saucepan. Add the hydrated chiles, ½ cup almonds, ¼ cup raisins, ¼ cup pumpkin seeds, and all the spices. Cook until almost dry. Add the water reserved from the chiles and the chocolate. Bring to a simmer and cook for 30 minutes. Place mixture in food processor and blend to your taste, a bit chunky or completely smooth.

To cook pork and mole: Place mole mixture in crock pot with pork shoulder and cook for approximately 2 hours till pork is tender.

To serve: Chop remaining ½ cup almonds, ¼ cup pumpkin seeds, and ¼ cup raisins and sprinkle on each serving as garnish. Sprinkle with toasted sesame seeds.

Grilled Skirt or Hanger Steak with Coffee Rub

SERVES 4

Hanger and skirt steak cuts have finally arrived in North America. In France, I loved "steak frîtes" with thin cuts of marbleized beef, unlike the big fat cuts of American steaks. Especially at places like The Meat Market in Great Barrington, you can easily order a cut of skirt steak. I even find it in my local supermarket.

2 pounds skirt or hanger steak

To prepare: Using clean hands, rub the steak with the Coffee Rub. Wrap in plastic or put in ziplock bag and place in refrigerator for a few hours to marinate. On the hottest grill, quickly grill the steak for a few minutes on each side. This cut of steak is thin and will cook quickly in 2–3 minutes on each side. Let rest and slice.

Coffee Rub

MAKES 2 OUNCES

This is a short-term solution for a coffee rub to add to meat or vegetables until you can order the very special Pierce Brothers' Coffee Rub. It took them two years to perfect it! (www.Piercebros coffee.com)

The basics:
1 tablespoon espresso grind of a quality coffee
2 tablespoons chile powder
1 tablespoon light brown sugar
1 tablespoon black pepper, preferably coarse ground

Optional additions:
½ teaspoon cayenne powder
1½ teaspoons paprika
½ teaspoon cumin

To make the rub: Mix all ingredients in a small bowl.

To apply the rub: Use hands to rub onto food or add enough olive oil (½ cup) to make a liquid spread and then apply the rub, using a pastry or basting brush, to meat, fish, or vegetables.

Note: You can let the spice soak in for a while or cook your food right away. The spice radiates even without marinating.

Desserts

Pear Clafoutis

SERVES 8

Clafoutis is a traditional French fruit dessert originally made with black cherries. The recipe is an adaptable, magic formula for making a fruit dessert without a lot of work, since there is no pastry involved. You can use almost any fruit: apples, cranberries, prunes, apricots, over which you will pour a liquid that cooks into a delicate flan-like custard. Clafoutis are easy, elegant, and delicious.

Equipment: 9-inch diameter and 1½-inch deep baking pan (pie, quiche pan, or cast-iron pan)

3–4 pears, ripe but firm
⅓ cup granulated sugar
1 tablespoon kirsch, Cognac, or almond extract
⅔ cup ground almonds or white flour
⅛ teaspoon salt

1 cup light cream
¼ cup milk
3 eggs, beaten

To prepare the fruit: Cut pears in half and then cut into thin slices (unpeeled if skin is tender). Place pears in shallow pan and add kirsch and sugar.

To prepare the custard: Put dry ingredients, ground almonds and salt, in one bowl. Place wet ingredients, cream, milk, eggs, in another bowl. Add wet to dry ingredients and blend with a whisk, or put in a blender.

To prepare baking pan: Arrange pears in a circular pattern, like the spokes of a wooden wheel. Pour the liquid mixture over the pears. **Note:** Stop pouring liquid if it starts to cover the tops of the pears. You want to be able to see the spiral pattern of the pears.

To bake: Place in oven at 375°F for about 60 minutes, until the surface is puffy and nicely browned.

To serve: Sprinkle powdered confectioners' sugar over the top. Serve clafoutis warm with spoonful of crème fraîche, Greek-style yogurt, or ice cream.

Almond Tart

This tart features great texture and contrast between the sweet pastry crust and chewy almond interior. Any sweetness in the filling is counterbalanced with the slightly "sour" nutty flavor. The dessert is ideal to bring to someone's house when you are asked to "just bring a dessert," because it transports well. It will be appreciated by the guests and it will be eaten, even the crumbs. (Is there anything worse than bringing home your contribution to the potluck, uneaten?) The tart may travel well, but there is no reason not to make it at home, a lot. Once you conquer "blind baking" a pastry shell, you can substitute endless fillings—all sorts of summer fruits—to place in it.

Equipment: 10-inch tart pan with fluted sides and removable bottom

For the pastry shell:

1 cup flour

1 tablespoon sugar

¼ teaspoon salt

3 to 4 drops vanilla extract

½ cup butter, cut into small pieces

⅓ cup cold water

For the filling:

¾ cup cream

¾ cup sugar

1 teaspoon Grand Marnier

3 drops almond extract

1½ cups sliced almonds, preferably with skins

To make pastry shell: Place flour, sugar, salt, and vanilla extract in bowl and add butter. Cut butter with two knives in criss-crossing manner or use your fingers to break up butter until it is the size of small peas. Add water gradually until the dough will gather into a ball. Knead a few times on a floured surface and then chill in refrigerator for a couple of hours.

To blind bake the shell: Roll out the dough until it is bigger than your greased tart pan. Fold dough in half and place in pan. Unfold and press into bottom and fluted sides of pan. Run the rolling pin across the top to evenly cut off the dough overhanging the edges. Prick bottom slightly but don't break through the dough or the filling will leak. Line the dough with a piece of aluminum foil and place small dry beans or lentils in the pan to support the sides while the tart bakes.

To bake: Bake the tart in a preheated oven at 350°F. Take tart from oven, remove beans and aluminum foil. Bake a few minutes longer until the bottom is brown. Let pastry shell cool.

To make tart filling: Mix cream, sugar and flavorings in heavy-bottom saucepan, large enough to contain the liquid when it triples in volume. Cook over high heat until the liquid comes to a rolling boil and becomes thicker. Add almonds to liquid. Remove pan from heat and let stand 15 minutes.

To bake: Pour filling into blind-baked tart shell. Smooth top with wet spatula. Place aluminum foil on bottom of oven because liquid tends to bubble up and spill over sides. Bake 25–30 minutes in a 375°F preheated oven until the almonds are a caramel color.

To serve: Allow to cool until it is easy to cut the tart.

Restaurants

Wheatleigh

Executive Chef: Jeffrey Thompson
Lenox

In 1893, Henry H. Cook commissioned a house in Lenox, Massachusetts, to replicate a sixteenth-century Florentine palazzo. This magnificent house, to be called Wheatleigh, was just a little gift for his daughter from wealthy "Daddy," Henry Cook, who had made a fortune in finance and railroads. The occasion of the gift was to honor his daughter, Georgie, on her marriage to Carlos de Heredia, a Spanish count. In the golden era at the turn of the century, industrialists, financiers, and tycoons were making lots of money and building pseudo-European palaces in places like the Berkshires. In the case of the Cook family, Georgie's wedding brought a noble title into the already rich family. Fortunately, Wheatleigh was built with a restrained style, not with the excesses of other palaces of the nouveau riche. One hundred and fifty artisans were imported from Italy to the Berkshires to build the estate. Under the guidance of the Boston architectural firm of Peabody and Stearns, these artisans laid marble floors and carved handsome detailing throughout the house. The famous landscape architect Frederick Law Olmsted, who designed New York's Central Park, was hired to create a park around the house. Wheatleigh was staffed with forty servants who kept the house open for six weeks in the summer, when their owners hosted dinners and music festivities. For the rest of the year, the 380 acres served as a working farm.

Today the house has been tastefully converted into one of the smallest hotels in the Relais and Chateaux group, with only nineteen rooms. There are several spaces in the hotel to dine.

There is a handsome wood-paneled dining space and a large great-room space with mirrors and a piano. Windows afford beautiful views of the hills. Diners can choose a la carte or tasting menus. The library serves casual food. In the summer when Tanglewood is in full swing, Wheatleigh offers a barbecue on the terrace each Wednesday night, with oysters, clams, corn, steak and other offerings that raise barbecue to another level. Guests can listen to live jazz before walking over to Tanglewood to attend a concert. Wheatleigh can also be rented for corporate events and weddings.

Wheatleigh is privately owned and operated by Lin and Susan Simon, who purchased the property

in 1981. They hired the architectural firm of Tsao and McKown to restore and renovate the house. The architects respected the strong bones of the house with large spaces, such as a big, open staircase with a two-story Tiffany window. The architects added antiques to highlight certain areas but the overall look of Wheatleigh is quasi-contemporary—clean and rich.

The hotel brings staff from Europe to apprentice and work at Wheatleigh, which adds a very sophisticated element. It is interesting to talk to the staff and learn about their country of origin and other hotels where they have worked. The weekend destination-wedding I attended at Wheatleigh was magical—the bride and groom arrived in a horse-drawn surrey that pulled into the walled front courtyard with its ornate fountain and wonderful wrought-iron work in the decorative canopy over and around the doorway. Dinner was served in a dining room with glass panels set in a bronze framework from where we could watch the sun set. Later there were fireworks and dancing to music played by musicians from the Boston Symphony Orchestra borrowed from Tanglewood.

One of the main attractions at Wheatleigh is Executive Chef Jeffrey Thompson. He doesn't come with the usual pedigree. Jeffrey laughs and says, "I didn't grow up living over the family restaurant in Europe. I was an all-American boy more interested in sports than cooking until I took a job as a dishwasher at the grand hotel The Broadmoor, in my hometown of Colorado Springs. At the time, an Austrian chef named Eisenberger was creating a new style of cuisine in the dining room, which got my attention. I was really lucky that Chef Eisenberger gave me an opportunity to cook in the kitchen." In fact, Eisenberger recognized Jeffrey's work ethic and ability to learn quickly and eagerly. Chef Eisenberger essentially gave Jeffrey a three-year apprenticeship, allowing him to practice at different stations in the kitchen. Jeffrey climbed the ladder and became the sous chef to Eisenberger, a position he held for four years. Then Jeffrey did a stint on the West Coast, worked at a restaurant in Williamsburg, Virginia, and finally joined the staff at Wheatleigh as the sous chef. Four years later, he was elevated to executive chef.

Jeffrey's food is inventive. With a tomato, he might create a tomato sorbet with a tomato-flavored cookie. When I visited Wheatleigh for the photo shoot, Jeffrey had prepared some elegant dishes using kampachi. Kampachi is sustainably raised in ocean waters in Hawaii, which produces safe, healthy, high-quality fish. In these recipes, Jeffrey prepared the fish raw as carpaccio and cooked the belly and jaw of the fish into another extraordinary dish. The various ingredients included *yuzu* aioli, diced watermelon radish, *shiso* (a Japanese herb), heart-of-palm slices, and citrus vinaigrette. Every dish is presented with colors, textures, and shapes that look way too elegant to disturb and a presentation that makes you want to photograph the dish for a lifetime memory. Jeffrey's cuisine is provocative and inventive.

Call Wheatleigh if you are interested in studying cooking with Jeffrey. He offers two types of cooking classes: those arranged around a theme and type of food he enjoys cooking (brunch menus, homemade pasta) and private lessons for students, where the students request recipes they wish to learn. Classes for children and wine and Champagne lessons are also offered. Wheatleigh is an elegant place to dine or sleep. Its location close to Tanglewood makes it the perfect place to stay in the Berkshires.

Apple Mustard Sorbet

SERVES 4

This recipe will zing your taste buds. It is a typical Jeffrey innovation. You expect a sweet apple sorbet but the mustard injects a tangy balance. The taste will be unfamiliar. You'll love it.

Equipment: Candy thermometer and sorbet machine

For the sorbet base:

½ pound apples, peeled and chopped

⅓ cup sugar

2 (5–6 ounce) cans apple juice

9 ounces water

8 teaspoons lemon juice

1 thyme sprig, leaves removed

1 bay leaf

For the sorbet:

2 teaspoons sugar

1 teaspoon sorbet stabilizer, such as Base Divina brand

5½ cups sorbet base (above)

½ (6-ounce) jar green apple mustard (order online if not available locally)

To prepare sorbet base: Put all ingredients in heavy, medium-size saucepan and cook till apples are tender. Puree in food processor and pass through a sieve.

To continue: Mix sugar and sorbet stabilizer (helps reduce ice crystals). Measure sorbet base and add. Cook in heavy-bottom saucepan until temperature reaches 185°F (85°C) on candy thermometer. Add the mustard and chill overnight.

Next day: Process in sorbet machine according to directions.

Onion Soup

SERVES 4

Jeffrey created this modern, light version from the foundations of the classic French onion soup recipe. Much of the credit is tied to Jeffrey's use of cipollini onions, which give the soup a mild, pleasantly sweet flavor. He also uses chicken, not beef, stock, which brings the soup up one level in lightness. From a top barista, I learned that nonfat milk foams better than whole milk or cream, and Jeffrey suggests the same trick here—use nonfat milk in the soup's recipe to froth correctly at the final stage. A touch of lemon adds acidity to balance the sweetness of the onions.

Equipment: 4–6 oven-safe soup bowls, such as the typical dark brown and beige French onion soup bowls with a handle

For the soup:

8 medium cipollini onions, peeled and sliced
½ cup canola oil
1½ cups dry white wine
2 sprigs thyme, leaves pulled off and chopped
2 bay leaves
1 quart chicken stock
1 cup nonfat milk
Lemon juice and salt and pepper to taste

For the topping:

1 baguette
½ pound gruyère cheese, grated (medium)
Cayenne pepper

To prepare: Cook onions in oil in a heavy-bottom saucepan until they are slightly brown and caramelized. Add white wine, thyme, and bay leaves and cook down until the liquid is nearly dry. Add chicken stock and simmer for 15 minutes, then pour milk into pan and puree the soup with a hand-held blender. Adjust with lemon juice and salt and pepper to your taste.

Meanwhile, cut slices of crusty baguette, toast pieces, cover with grated gruyère cheese and sprinkle with a bit of cayenne pepper.

To serve: Ladle soup into individual bowls and place on cookie sheet. Top each with slice of bread with cheese and place in 500°F oven or under broiler till cheese melts and bread toasts. Be careful, since the cheese will burn quickly.

Coco and The Cellar Bar

Owners and Chefs: Unmi Abkin and Roger Taylor
Easthampton

The co-owners of the restaurant Coco and The Cellar Bar, Unmi Abkin and Roger Taylor, have created a very special restaurant in the Pioneer Valley. What attracts me to their food is that they have drilled deep to find a way to present simple foods that ring true to their ingredients. I immediately thought of the Japanese concept *wabi sabi* when I ate their food. This Japanese term is used to describe an aesthetic that connotes rustic simplicity, freshness or quietness, and an understated elegance. That is exactly it. When you experience Coco's food, it seems simple but you realize it is not simple. An element of surprise and freshness in each dish makes you understand that you are experiencing an understated elegance.

I am impressed with the fact that Roger and Unmi achieved this quality in their food. Roger chuckles when he describes "certain restaurants that try to impress customers with their big fold-out menus and descriptions of foods that go on for a paragraph." Some of these restaurants manipulate foods for taste and presentation following a trend by chefs to cook foods in extravagant, innovative ways "just because you can." Roger's reflection is that "usually quality has to suffer" and when the restaurant keeps three full pages of foods from these fold-out menu on hand for the occasional person who orders that dish, "lots of food is wasted." Roger is grateful for his cooking experiences at several highly rated restaurants but in many ways, he says, it also drove him and Unmi in the opposite direction. "We are stripping down the dishes to the essentials, to create pure tastes with a limited menu and at an affordable price."

Roger mentions the limited menu was driven, a bit, by space. Coco's kitchen only has six burners to cook for as many as sixty people. But it was really a philosophical approach that drove Unmi and Roger to produce a thoughtful, small menu. Don't confuse small with easy. Unmi is constantly reading and learning and trying new ways of making food that is "lighter and brighter." When Unmi decided to make a curry, she studied curries and cooked curries, tasted curries and lived curries. Unmi was searching to understand the essence of exactly what she needed to put in her curry and how to prepare it. Rather than trying to imitate a Thai curry, Unmi was striving to make her own version. She was able to buy superb Thai chiles from a local farm, Kitchen Garden. Then she experimented. One trick that is basic to a fine curry, she discovered, is to grind the spices with a mortar and pestle. Electric food blenders and processors can't synthesize the flavors. Then Unmi adds her own unexpected surprise touch. She serves the Thai curry with wide Chinese rice noodles. Unmi found a way to deliver the "real" flavor of curry with that subtle element of surprise.

Just as they do their utmost to bring the perfect balance to their food, Roger and Unmi are attempting to achieve a balance in their lives. Roger jokes, "Some people say we live the laziest life because the restaurant is only open four nights a week, but we are working on the days when we aren't in the restaurant to make the experience of our customers be the best it can be on those four nights. We spend four days at the restaurant all day. I usually take our daughter to school and Unmi spends the entire day at the restaurant. I often pick up Coco [their daughter], who comes to the restaurant with us. She might eat at the restaurant or Unmi will take her home for dinner. Then I spend the whole evening at the restaurant cooking. When the restaurant is open we have to juggle our lives and we felt that it was critical to have three days to live like a normal family. Food is our lives but so is our life as a family."

Roger and Unmi's journey to opening their restaurant Coco combines East and West Coast experiences. Unmi, Korean by birth, was adopted at an early age by a Mexican Roman Catholic mother and a father of Russian Jewish heritage. She grew up in California, spending her summers in Mexico. For college, she attended UC Santa Cruz and Le Cordon Bleu College of Culinary Arts in San Francisco. Unmi also completed an internship at the iconic Chez Panisse.

Roger was raised "in the restaurant business, whipping cream or squeezing lemons as a child to help my father and cousin in a local Amherst, Massachusetts, restaurant called Lone Wolf. As an adult, Roger headed to California and worked at the two-star Los Angeles restaurant Melisse, and later at Pizzaiolo, the Oakland restaurant opened by a chef who worked at Chez Panisse for twenty years. Roger met Unmi when they were both at College of Culinary Arts.

After they met, Unmi reached into her Mexican heritage and her Mexican summers with relatives and developed, according to Roger's account, "the brilliant idea of opening a burrito restaurant." ChaChaCha opened in Northampton and was wildly successful. When Unmi opened another restaurant, a fine dining establishment, Roger was her sous chef. Soon, they realized they weren't looking for a theme restaurant or elegant dining. They were looking for something else. So, they closed the restaurants, pondered and reflected. In September of 2011, they opened Coco.

Roger says, "Sure, I am a great cook, but Unmi is the creative genius and force behind the food. I am more of a nuts and bolts man and I am happy to let my wife take the lead. She eats, dreams, and lives food. She might even wake up in the middle of the night and tell me that she just realized what was wrong with some recipe she was reading in a cookbook at a Barnes and Noble store weeks before. Unmi's role is developing and perfecting foods for the restaurant." The menu doesn't change often and when a new dish is introduced, it is done gradually. Roger leaves it to Unmi to "decide what and when. We can't abandon our loyal customers who love our fried chicken or the miso noodles for just $11, but we are continually seeking and endeavoring to find new and better foods."

At first, the restaurant only occupied the upstairs space while the lower level continued to be rented out as a bar. Soon, they were able to take over the lease for the bar as well and combine the two places into Coco and The Cellar Bar. Unmi loved the challenge of making cocktails. "It's like building blocks. The same as in cooking. One ingredient after another until you get the right balance, the best yin-yang." Unmi is looking for a fantastic combination of ingredients in the restaurant offerings and she puts the same effort into creating cocktails.

Roger proudly explains "While 99 percent of the bars in America use pale sugary tonic water as the base for cocktails, Unmi makes her own tonic water." Then she plays with ingredients and herbs to achieve her "lighter brighter" goal. Unmi will work with Japanese *yuzu* or a Prohibition-era Caribbean cocktail syrup called falernum. Unmi even works with a forager who gathers dozens of herbs, grinds and seeps them in a mild vodka until the flavor and character of the herbs emerge. Then Unmi takes this brilliant chartreuse liquid and makes cocktails that respect the base herbs. Unmi works in a partnership with Roger's sister, who is in charge of The Cellar Bar and front of the house.

Last of all, why are the restaurant and Roger and Unmi's child both called Coco? It is the nickname given to Roger's father during World War II when he was put on a boat for a three-week ocean voyage to the South Pacific. He'd never been on a boat before and had no idea that he would become seriously seasick and unable to keep food or water in his body. His medical condition was turning dangerous until a doctor discovered that Roger's father was able to abide the drink Coca-Cola. After that, he was given the nickname, "Coke" or "Coco," and it stuck with him his whole life. It is common to name a child for a family member and in this case, little Coco is proud of her unusual name, and she is equally proud that the restaurant is named for both her and her grandfather. That is a pretty neat story. I encourage you to explore the restaurant behind the name Coco and taste its exceptional, genuine food.

Honey Miso Noodles

SERVES 5–6

Unmi and Roger, with a little help from Coco, serve this delicious noodle dish, which is perfect for spring since Unmi interprets it with "light and bright flavors." The one-bowl noodle dish is (amazingly) reasonably priced and a favorite at the restaurant Coco and The Cellar Bar. Visit this hidden gem and try other dishes. Unmi and Roger especially created and tested a smaller home-size portion of this recipe and are sharing it with you.

For the noodles:

4 cups wide Chinese egg noodles, cooked

1½ cups diced, cooked chicken breast

2 cups shredded carrots

4 cups shredded napa cabbage

3 tablespoons chopped cilantro

3 cups arugula

For the dressing:

2 tablespoons white miso

¼ cup seasoned rice wine vinegar

1 tablespoons soy sauce

1½ tablespoons honey

¼ teaspoon sesame oil

1 teaspoon minced garlic

1 teaspoon minced ginger

½ cup canola oil

For the garnish:

6 scallions, chopped

2 teaspoons crushed red pepper

2 tablespoons toasted sesame seeds

To prepare noodles: Cook egg noodles according to directions. In a large bowl, toss to combine noodles and chicken with carrots, cabbage, cilantro, and arugula.

To prepare dressing: Whisk together first seven ingredients (all the ingredients except canola oil), then slowly whisk in canola oil to emulsify. Pour dressing lightly over noodle, chicken, and vegetable mixture and toss gently.

To serve: Divide noodles among six bowls and garnish with scallions, red pepper, and sesame seeds.

Food Producers

Peace Valley Farm

Owners: Bill and Susan Stinton
Williamstown

Bill Stinton, the owner of Peace Valley Farm, is a guru, one of the first pioneers in sustainable farming in the Berkshires, who has influenced a whole generation of young people and changed the culture of food. Peace Valley Farm, an idyllic farm in Williamstown, has close ties with Williams College, which is located in the same town. In 2000, influenced by the farm-to-table movement, Williams College made a commitment to purchase as much local produce as possible. Peace Valley Farm jumped on the bandwagon and ever since has been working closely with the chefs and managers of Dining Services to provide the highest quality foods to the students, faculty, and college guests. In return for being able to sell 55 percent of their produce to the college, Peace Valley Farm gives priority to Williams students who wish to intern at the farm during the summer.

Actually, Farmer Stinton's relationship with Williams College started even earlier—in the 1980s, when Bill Stinton would sell, at very little cost, Peace Valley's excess produce to the college. In the 1990s, Peace Valley Farm took its first Williams College intern, and approximately sixty students have interned on the farm since then. Many of the students live with Susan and Bill Stinton in their home.

One of my favorite examples of a link between Williams College and Peace Valley Farm is a college program called "Where Am I?," an annual bus tour of the Berkshires that orients students to the rich region and includes a stop at Peace Valley Farm to pick fingerling potatoes. When these potatoes are cooked and served in all the dining rooms for the Harvest Dinner, there is "intense excitement behind the golden nugget," says one of the students who helped bring the farm to the table, in other words, Peace Valley Farm to Williams College.

It hasn't been an easy road for the Stintons. Bill encountered every imaginable challenge as he carved an agricultural life out of New England woods over the past thirty years. Accidents, pests, and bad weather were only some of the trials. Bill built the farm from the ground up—literally. He created fertile land from the rocky soil of the northern Berkshires. Year after year Farmer Stinton added composted organic farm waste, plus leaf matter donated by Williams College. Now the soil is fecund and rich. Productivity has been increased by adding solar energy and greenhouses with raised beds to allow the farm to grow all sorts of crops without the use of pesticides or herbicides. The farmland remains the same size as when the Stintons originally bought the land thirty years ago from a longtime Berkshire resident, but the Stintons have been able to dramatically increase the productivity of the land.

All this toil has paid off. Today people are asking about the origins of their food and turn to places like Peace Valley Farm where they can trust that the produce has been grown in a sustainable manner. In the "old days," Bill says, "we were way ahead of the curve and were cut out of supplying food to restaurants and institutions because we weren't the big industrialized supplier. Nobody wanted us." Now, not only does Bill supply food to Williams College, but also to other institutions, including a local hospital and several fine restaurants, like Mezze and the Williams Inn. He also sells at the farmers' markets, which have become popular due to the contemporary interest in food.

Bill finds the most exciting part of sharing his farming methods and philosophy is the enthusiasm with which younger people are embracing how food is grown. Bill has become a celebrity for these students. Through their contact with Bill and work on Peace Valley Farm, young people have come to fully appreciate the honest, dirty toil of farming, as well as seeing their mission as greater than farming alone. Farming is a political act. It is a means of influencing the corporate dominance over the food supply and society. For the student interns like those from Williams College, "Farming is a heroic effort to save us from the worst excesses of capitalism. Farmers have become the protagonists in a morality tale about saving society from itself. It is little wonder that farmers are the unlikely rock stars of the movement," says Katherine Gustafson in her new book, *Change Comes to Dinner.*

Bill is happy to know that some of the Williams College interns will become farmers, but Bill believes all of them have learned about food and farming—and why sustainable farming is good for the body, the mind, and the universe. "Each student learns about farming, small business practices, teamwork, and respect for the land." Bill and Susie Stinton started out with a modest personal effort—to grow clean and healthy food—and have ended up appealing to numerous college-age students, and people of all ages, concerned about finding an authentic way of living that respects the environment and makes them feel good about their work. Congratulations to everyone.

Hancock Shaker Village

Pittsfield

Hancock Shaker Village is an outdoor living museum on 750 acres with twenty authentic buildings, including my favorite—a circular stone barn. With a gentle, peaceful atmosphere reflecting the Shaker philosophy, the village beckons you to wander at your own pace into some of the historic buildings or to observe staff demonstrating Shaker crafts; enjoy the landscape or watch the farmers tending livestock; or visit the museum, cafe or store. Go to www.hancockshakervillage.com for a list of all the village's activities. Spring and summer are favorite seasons because of all the baby animals born on the farm. Every fall there is an October Shaker Supper, which features cider and cheese, followed by a candlelight dinner, but there are fascinating things to see and do in every season. The village is closed in the winter but there are some scheduled tours and activities.

The eighteenth-century Shaker community that was established in the Berkshires was a forerunner of today's local and sustainable food movement. Shakers utilized organic agricultural techniques that respected the land, and yet they were constantly seeking the latest scientific methods and inventing new methods to achieve better results. The Shakers raised all their own food, were the first large producers of medicine in the United States, and were the first to save and sell seeds in paper packets. Their furniture and architecture have had a lasting effect on American design. This religion has nearly died out, but the Shakers left their footprint and legacy for you to marvel at in this extraordinary village.

A religious sect founded in England in 1774, the Shakers came to America seeking religious freedom. Their religious tenets were based on racial and gender equality, simplicity, pacifism, celibacy, communal life, and confession of sins. They performed ecstatic religious services in which they "shook off" their sins, and this caused them to be named "Shakers," for the trembling and whirling they exhibited when worshipping. One of the most successful utopian communities established in America, the Shakers numbered around five thousand by the mid-nineteenth century, although the Shaker communities have almost died out, with only a few elder Shakers alive. Sometime ridiculed for their tenet of celibacy, which would obviously doom the community, the Shakers expected adoption and conversion of unwanted children to perpetuate their communities. Though there was religious questioning and social turmoil in America in the early nineteenth century, there were never enough converts to perpetuate their sect.

Hancock Shaker Village is rich with interpretive tours, craft and cooking demonstrations, lectures and workshops, and Shaker-inspired food from the farm served at the Village Harvest Cafe. The Children's Discovery Room invites children to try weaving a chair seat, weave on a loom, try on Shaker clothes, and milk a replica of a cow. The baby animals, including many heritage breeds, are fascinating for both children and adults.

With over 22,000 examples of Shaker furniture, crafts, tools, and clothing, Hancock Shaker Village is a rich archive of Shaker life and design. The Shaker creed stated, "Beauty rests in the utility. Let it be plain and simple, of

good substantial quality, and unencumbered by any superfluities. . . ." As a result, Shakers created exquisitely spare objects with serenity and grace that still draw admiration from visitors to the Hancock Shaker Village. It is easy to spend several days visiting this living museum if you want to experience even a small portion of their offerings. Food lovers will enjoy the medicinal and produce gardens, the farm and gardening tools, and Shaker food in the cafe. But everyone, food lover or not, can enjoy this gem.

Shaker Lemon Pie

SERVES 8

Since sources of vitamin C were scarce in nineteenth-century Pioneer Valley, the Shaker communities made lemon pies to prevent scurvy. Enjoy this historic tart recipe and think of it as a way of taking your daily vitamins, not as eating a dessert. The pie easily rivals a lemon meringue yet is much easier to make. It has a tart flavor and slightly chewy texture from the whole lemons.

Equipment: 8–9 inch pie pan

For the crust:
3½ cups all-purpose unbleached flour
¼ teaspoon salt
¾ cup butter
¼ cup water, cold with ice cubes
(Or buy one 8-inch frozen prepared pie shell)

For the filling:
4 large lemons
2 cups granulated sugar
¼ teaspoon salt
4 large eggs, plus one yolk

For the glaze:
½ cup milk
1 egg

Step #1 or Day 1

To prepare the lemons: Wash and cut two of the lemons into thin slices. Remove peel and pith of the remaining two lemons; slice the fleshy, juicy part into chunks and put them with the thin lemon slices in a large mixing bowl. Add sugar and salt and toss well to coat. Cover bowl and set aside for 4 hours or overnight.

To make pie dough: Put flour and salt into bowl. Add butter cut into small pieces. Break up butter quickly with hands till pea size. Add cold water as needed, until flour-butter mixture will gather together. Divide into two pieces. Cover and chill 2 hours or overnight.

Step #2 or Day 2

To prepare the filling: Beat eggs and yolk with fork or electric mixer. Add eggs to lemon mixture and mix. Set aside until pie shell is ready.

To prepare pie crusts: Roll out one ball of dough on floured surface until slightly larger than a pie pan. Fold dough in half and place in greased pie pan. Unfold and lightly press to fit it into pan.

To complete pie: Place lemon filling in pie shell. Roll out second ball of dough and cut big enough to go slightly over edges of pie pan. Place dough over the pie filling. Crimp edges to seal top and bottom crusts together. Use fork to make a few perforations in the top crust to release steam.

To glaze: Put milk in small bowl, add egg and whip with fork. Use pastry brush to apply over surface and edges of pie.

To bake: Preheat oven to 450°F and brush top of pie with egg-milk mixture. Bake 15 minutes, reduce heat to 375°F, and bake for another 30 minutes. Cool before cutting and serving.

Farm Recipes

Pestos

Ever a traditionalist, I only used to make pesto with basil and pine nuts. When my friend Gabriel noticed all the bolted arugula and mâche lettuces in my garden, she suggested I use them to make pesto. What a revelation. Almost any small-leafed green vegetable can be converted to pesto. Although I am fond of pine nuts due to my father's time living in the Middle East, I mainly use walnuts, due to the cost. Experiment and see what pesto sauce you like.

Carrot Top Pesto

YIELDS 1¼ CUPS

½ cup pine nuts or walnuts, toasted
2 cups carrot leaves, stems removed and coarsely chopped
¾ cup olive oil
2 large garlic cloves
½ teaspoon salt
½ cup grated Parmesan cheese

To prepare nuts: Spread nuts in a single layer on a rimmed pan. Place in 350°F oven and toast till lightly brown, 5–10 minutes, or roast in heavy-bottom frying pan. Watch carefully because they will burn quickly.

To make pesto: Place carrot leaves, oil, garlic, and salt in food processor. Pulse till finely minced. Add nuts and pulse again. Add Parmesan and pulse. Taste and adjust seasonings or oil. Use or cover and refrigerate.

Roasted Pepper Pesto

YIELDS 2 CUPS

Roasting or charring peppers transforms a crunchy vegetable into a sweet, soft one. You can also buy jars of roasted peppers, which will save you a step.

2 large roasted red bell peppers (you can use yellow or orange roasted peppers too!)
1 tablespoon fresh oregano or other herbs of your choice
2 cloves garlic
2 tablespoons pine nuts, toasted
2 tablespoons crumbled feta
2 tablespoons olive oil
2 teaspoons balsamic vinegar
Salt and pepper to taste

To roast peppers: Cut peppers in half lengthwise. Cover broiler pan in aluminum foil and place peppers on pan. Press down on peppers to flatten them. Broil, turning pan occasionally, until peppers are charred. Let peppers sit for 12–15 minutes to soften, then remove charred skin of peppers. Rinse under water to remove stray skin.

To prepare: Place all ingredients in a food processor and puree. Save in lidded container.

Basil Pesto

YIELDS 3 CUPS

2 cups basil leaves, loosely packed
2 medium cloves garlic, chopped
½ cup olive oil
½ teaspoon salt
½ cup grated Parmesan cheese
½ cup pine nuts, toasted in dry skillet over medium heat
    for 2–3 minutes

To prepare: Put garlic in food processor and pulse. Add basil, then stream in olive oil while running food processor. Add salt, Parmesan, and pine nuts. Puree and save in tight lidded container.

Parsley Pesto

YIELDS 3½ CUPS

2 cloves garlic
1 cup coarsely chopped walnuts
2 cups parsley leaves, loosely packed
½ cup olive oil
2 teaspoons lemon juice
½ teaspoon salt

To prepare: Put garlic in food processor and pulse. Add walnuts, parsley and stream in olive oil while running food processor. Add lemon juice and salt. Save in lidded container.

Chicken Enchiladas

SERVES 8

Cricket Creek Farm, Williamstown

This is a recipe that works well with one of Cricket Creek Farm's "spent" laying hens (hens that are no longer laying eggs) as it will impart a stronger chicken flavor. The long, slow cooking in this recipe suits an older, tougher chicken's meat well. Maggie's Round, Cricket Creek Farm's award-winning cheese, is perfect for this recipe, but any good sharp cheese is fine. Take a Berkshire bird and add a Mexican twist.

1 small whole chicken

Salt

1 onion, finely diced

2 garlic cloves, minced

1 large or 2–3 small spicy chile peppers (habanero, jalapeño, poblano), seeded and minced

2 tablespoons olive oil

3 large ripe tomatoes, diced

Cumin

Fresh or dried oregano

1 tablespoon brown sugar

1 cup water

12 ounces good sharp cheese, shredded

16 corn tortillas

Sour cream

Avocado

5 sprigs cilantro, stems removed, leaves minced

To prepare: Cover the whole chicken with salted water by at least 2 inches in a heavy stockpot. Bring to a simmer and cook until the meat is cooked through, about 30–45 minutes. Remove from pot and shred chicken into a bowl. (Reduce and save the water for chicken soup!)

To make sauce: Cook the onion, garlic, and chiles in saucepan with olive oil, until the onion is translucent. Add the tomatoes, spices, and sugar to taste. Bring to a boil, then lower to a simmer. Place in a food processor with 1 cup water and blend.

To assemble: Combine the shredded chicken, half the shredded cheese, and half of the sauce in a large mixing bowl. Distribute this filling evenly among 16 corn tortillas, then roll the tortillas and place in a 9 x 12-inch baking dish. The tortillas may fall apart, but since they are in a casserole dish, they can be scooped out easily.

To bake: Distribute the remaining cheese and sauce on top of the tortillas and bake, covered, in a 350°F oven for at least 45 minutes or until the cheese is bubbling and the edges of the tortillas begin to crisp. Serve hot with sour cream, avocado, and fresh cilantro.

Locally Sourced Banh Mi Sandwich

Simple Gifts Farm, Amherst
Farm Managers: Dave Tepfer and Jeremy Plotkin

YIELDS 1 LARGE SANDWICH

Dave Tepfer, Jeremy Plotkin, and their families are stewards of Simple Gifts, a land trust that is a farm, wildlife corridor, community resource with walking trails, and educational project. The land trust was a heroic effort to save land and bring organic products to the local population. The farm offers their version of a Vietnamese sandwich.

In the late 1940s and early 1950s, when the French still had a heavy presence in Vietnam, a Vietnamese-French fusion sandwich evolved that combined a French baguette, mayonnaise, and butter with Vietnamese pickled vegetables, cilantro, nuoc mam (sauce from fermented fish), and chiles. Currently they have created quite a buzz in the US, including several cookbooks that call these sandwiches "crazy delicious."

Below is Simple Gifts Farm's recipe, using their choice of ingredients for this popular sandwich that they call "Locally Sourced Banh Mi Sandwich." Having lived in Vietnam for three years, I would like to suggest adding lettuce, mayonnaise, jalapeño chile slices, and thin slices of Persian-style cucumbers, too.

For the pickled vegetables:

3 cups warm water

6 tablespoons distilled or rice vinegar

¼ cup white sugar

2 tablespoons salt

½ pound carrots, sliced in thin matchstick strips

½ pound daikon radish, sliced in thin matchstick strips

For the sandwich and filling:

1 medium-small baguette, not too crunchy or difficult to eat

1 tablespoon unsalted butter, room temperature

2 cloves garlic, crushed

2 teaspoons sugar

2 tablespoons fish sauce (nuoc mam)

2 tablespoons ground black pepper

2 tablespoons onion or shallots, finely diced

¼ vegetable or grapeseed oil

1 teaspoon sesame seed oil

1 pound pork chop, shoulder or loin, thinly sliced

Condiments (my addition):

Mayonnaise and butter for baguette

Persian-style cucumbers, thinly sliced

Jalapeño pepper, deseeded and sliced

Lettuce, crispy type like romaine

To prepare vegetables: Mix warm water, vinegar, sugar, and salt until everything is dissolved. Put the mixture in a pitcher. Combine carrot and daikon strips in bowl, toss together, then place in jar. Pour vinegar mixture into jar till full. Close lid and let the vegetables pickle for 3–5 days, or until desired sourness is reached. For immediate use, let marinate for 1 hour.

To prepare pork: Mix all ingredients (except pork) in a plastic bag. Let all ingredients dissolve in oil, then add slices of pork. Allow everything to marinate at least 1 hour. Heat up frying pan, lay slices of pork down in pan, cook, and then flip to cook the other side. Repeat until all the pork is cooked.

To assemble: Cut small baguette in half lengthwise. Butter one side and spread mayonnaise on the other. Line thin slices of cucumbers, pepper, and the pickled vegetables on one half of the baguette and lettuce on the other half. Place pork on lettuce and close sandwich. Cut into pieces and share.

Crispy Garlic Scapes

SERVES 3–4

Farm Girl Farm, North Egremont and Great Barrington
Owner: Laura Meister
Recipe credit: Hannah Karcheski

Hannah Karcheski of Farm Girl Farm kindly donated her garlic scape recipe. I started growing garlic several years ago. I love garlic, but I think maybe I even love scapes better. Their taste is that of mild garlic blended with onion, and their curlicue shape is just endearing. These are a perfect accompaniment to grilled chicken and corn. They are also great chopped up after grilling and used as a garnish or "relish" for grilled meat, rice, or sautéed corn. Watch these grilled scapes disappear right before your eyes!

1 large bunch of garlic scapes (snap garlic stalk as you would an asparagus stalk to leave best portion, then cut off the "flower" or bud at the top)
1 small bunch scallions, cleaned, and trimmed of ⅓ of the greens at the end and the roots
Few tablespoons of canola or olive oil (not extra virgin)
Couple pinches of kosher salt
2–3 grinds of fresh pepper
Pinch of cayenne, paprika, and garlic powder (optional)

To prepare: Put scapes and scallions in a bowl or ziplock bag and drizzle with oil and dust with spices. Mix to meld flavors. These vegetables can stand by in this mixture for 1–2 hours if you're prepping and cooking other things for the grill.

For grilling: Preheat grill to medium. Place scapes and/or scallions directly onto grill, angling them across grate so they don't fall through. Cook, moving around often, for 10–15 minutes or so, until golden brown and tender. Taste one and see if you like the texture—some people like them a bit more al dente. Let cool slightly before digging in.

SUMMER TOUR

Lush and green are the two best adjectives to describe summer in the Berkshires and Pioneer Valley. Green grass, green fields, green trees. And lush, ripe red tomatoes, orange peppers and carrots, yellow squash and beets. The colors are glorious. The food is magnificent. Take your bike or car and begin to explore and fulfill your food fantasies.

Cricket Creek Farm, Williamstown

Cricket Creek Farm is mainly a dairy farm where you can watch and learn about cheesemaking. You will want to load up on their artisanal cheeses, little art forms unto themselves that are for sale at the farm store, along with meat from the farm (and insulated bags), eggs, and local food products like honey and yogurt. The farm store is self-service and runs on an honor system. In the summer, the young calves, pigs, and chicks will be running around the farm. With their farm store, Cricket Creek Farm obviously welcomes guests. If you want a tour, you can drop in unannounced but it is also nice to let the staff know you are coming. (413) 458-5888.

SUMMER TOUR

Nejaimes, Lenox

Secure tickets for a music event at Tanglewood and you can eat at the Tanglewood cafe/restaurant. A favorite tradition, though, is picnicking on the lawn while listening to music. So, stop at Nejaimes and buy fixings for a picnic or order one of their prepared picnics with foods paired with wine. Nejaimes is a premier wine and cheese store with highly knowledgeable staff (ask for Bob Luhman) who will describe and offer samplings of locally made cheeses.

Wheatleigh, Lenox

Dining is elegant at Wheatleigh (see profile), but if you want a more casual evening, make reservations for their Midsummer BBQ every Wednesday night between late June and early September. A family-style meal on the terrace, the BBQ offers all sorts of seafood like oysters, shrimp, and lobster plus meats like steak and lamb chops and grilled corn.

The People's Pint, Greenfield

While you are in the Pioneer Valley, visit this pub-with-ethics, located in the same small town as the Pierce Brothers Coffee warehouse. The People's Pint has a good supply of beers matched with tasty organic menu offerings. The owner feeds brewery waste to his pigs and restaurant compost is recycled and used in the gardens for vegetables to be served in the restaurant. Both the Berkshires and Pioneer Valley attract lots of bikers in the fall, where you can ride hills through unspoiled landscapes and farmlands. The People's Pint's owner treats bicyclists to discounts at this restaurant.

West End Pub, Shelburne Falls

Ask for a table on the deck of this cafe, where you will have a perfect view of the Bridge of Flowers. While at the cafe, try some of the local beers and one of its menu items, an interesting twist on coleslaw made with broccoli. If you are curious and ask your server, you might learn that in 1928 an abandoned bridge was transformed into a "garden in the air." A May plant sale is extremely popular for its quality seeds and plants from some of the best private gardens in the region.

Chez Albert, Amherst

Call ahead for a reservation at this upscale French restaurant featuring local produce such as Chef Paul's pâté and slow-cooked meats or, for spring, focus on his salads and local vegetables.

Coco and The Cellar Bar, Easthampton

After you read the profile on Coco and The Cellar Bar and look at the chef's recipes, you will be eager to try this restaurant or The Cellar Bar or *both*. Clean food with carefully constructed flavors. Reasonable and fun.

Price Chopper, Great Barrington

A supermarket? Really? Yes, stop and buy some of Ted Dobson's eighty different varieties of greens. Pack them in a cooler to take home and you can have the same deluxe microgreens usually only available in upscale restaurants in your home—direct from the supermarket. Drive by Ted's farm, Equinox in Sheffield, to admire the rows of different shades of green and endless textures that make up the hundreds of microgreens, lettuces, and herbs that grow in the fields.

Gould Farm, 100 Gould Road, Monterey

Monterey is close to Great Barrington. Stop at the Barn Bakery and Cafe on the weekend, 9–3, and buy some of the variety of baked goods and pastries, or other farm products like cheese, eggs, milk, and maple syrup. Dine at the cafe and support this residential farm, where clients are treated for psychosocial disorders in a residential therapeutic community and guests (clients), staff, and their families and volunteers live and farm together. Farmwork helps every client gain dignity, heal, and produce tasty produce to purchase.

Cook's Garden at Historic Deerfield, Deerfield

Historic Deerfield is far more interesting than many other historic villages because it retains its original town plan and scale and a dozen magnificent houses. The Cook's Garden, near the Visitors Center at the Hall Tavern,

supplies foods for open hearth demonstrations and serves as an educational tool for understanding herbs used in early American cooking. Enroll in cooking classes or attend lectures, such as one on corn (explaining Native Americans' and European colonists' use of corn and answering the question of why popcorn pops). With a self-guided tour, guests can enjoy history out of doors, including a historic farm. If you love antique furniture and decorative arts, visit the Flynt Center for Early American Life. There is truly something for every age and interest. Return in the fall to see this picturesque village in another season.

Hancock Shaker Village, Pittsfield

Glimpse a fascinating religious sect that has nearly died out. Visit the open-air museum with twenty historic buildings, including a magnificent circular stone barn, 22,000 examples of Shaker furniture, plus tools, historic gardens, farm animals, and 750 acres of land. Take advantage of interpretive tours, craft and cooking demonstrations, workshops, or visiting the animals.

Peace Valley Farm, Williamstown

Once you are in Pittsfield at the Shaker Village, it is not much farther to Williamstown, the location of Peace Valley Farm. Farmer Bill Stinton is a leader in sustainable agriculture and has mentored lots of Williams College students. It's a beautiful farm. Call ahead (413-458-4866) to let Bill and Susan Stinton know you would like to visit the farm.

Recipe Index

About the Author

Jane Barton Griffith is passionate about food—its origins; the effect of the Slow Food movement in preserving food traditions and building community; and the future environmental challenges of food production. Recently she lived and worked in the Berkshires at Berkshire Mountain Bakery, which is owned by master baker Richard Bourdon, who has been a mentor to bakers like Chad Robertson of Tartine. A longtime home baker, she turned her baking expertise into an instructional cookbook about making artisanal styles of breads in the book *Knead It*. Jane has worked and lived in the United States, Europe, and Southeast Asia, and traveled to fifty countries, where she enjoyed tasting a variety of foods, from street food to meals at finer restaurants. Some of her flavor memories influence the recipes in this book.

About the Photographer

Barbara Dowd's photographs communicate the beauty and pleasure she experiences in travel, nature, and excellent food. A former video producer and trainer, her current photographic work reflects her travels among the Native American ruins of the American Southwest as well as the coastal beauty of her home in Newburyport, MA. She exhibits at the Newburyport Art Association and the Parker River Photographic Society.